Arnhem 1944

Arnhem 1944

JANUSZ PIEKALKIEWICZ

Translated by H. A. and A. J. Barker

Charles Scribner's Sons
NEW YORK

First published in the German language as *'Arnhem 1944'* in 1976

© 1976 Verlag Gerhard AG, Oldenburg and Hamburg

Copyright under the Berne Convention

1 3 5 7 9 11 13 15 17 19 I/C 20 18 16 14 12 10 8 6 4 2

Printed in Great Britain

Library of Congress Catalog Card No 77-82242

ISBN 0-684-15479-X

Contents

Acknowledgements

For their friendly help I wish to express my sincere thanks to the following:

Dr M. Haupt and Herr H. Walther of the Bundesarchiv, Koblenz; Mr J. S. Lucas and Mr P. H. Reed and the staff of the Imperial War Museum, London; Col W. D. Kasprowics of the Zwiazek Polskich Spadochroniarzy, London; Commander J. Wronski, Capt W. Milewski, Capt R. Dembinski and Capt St. Zurakowski of the Sikorski Institute, London; Major G. G. Norton and S.Sgt T. H. Fitch, of the Airborne Forces Museum, Aldershot; Frau Dr v. Gersdorff of the Militärgeschichtliches Forschungsamt, Freiburg; Herr M. Meyer at the Militärarchiv, Freiburg; Mnr A. Groeneweg of the Bibliotheek Arnhem, and Mnr Ir. J. Voskuil, Oosterbeek.

Sources

Pilot's Notes for Horsa I Glider, Air Ministry, London, January 1944

Bittrich, W., *Kampfbericht des II. SS-Panzer-Korps, August-November 1944*

Bradley, O. N., *A Soldier's Story*, 1951

Brereton, L. H., *The Brereton Diaries*, 1946

By Air To Battle, Official Account of the British Airborne Division, London 1945

Dempsey, M., *Operations of the 2nd Army in Europe*, 1947

Eisenhower, D. D., *Crusade in Europe*, 1948

Harzer, W., *Die Mitwirkung der 9. SS-Pz. Div. (Kampfgruppe) an der Schlacht von Arnheim, 1944*

Horrocks, B., *A Full Life*, 1960

Iddekinge, drs. P. R. A. van, *Arnhem September 1944*, 1969

Intelligence Corps, *With the Airborne at Arnhem*. Notes of Interest, Vol. 8, 1945

Krafft, S., *Gefechtsbericht des SS-Pz. Gren.*, Ausb. u. Ers. Btl. 16, 1944

Model, W., *OKW-AGr. B, Kriegstagebuch, 1 Sept.-15. Okt. 1944*

Montgomery, B., *Normandy to the Baltic*, 1947

Polscy Spadochroniarze, Pamietnik Zolnierzy, 1947

Sosabowski, S., *Najkrotsza Droga*, 1957

Student, K., *Alliierte Luftlande-Unternehmen vom 17. September 1944*, 1944

Urquhart, R. E., *Arnhem*, 1958

Unpublished Allied Documents

1. Allied Airborne HQ
1. British Airborne Corps
1. British Airborne Division
82. US Airborne Division
101. US Airborne Division
1. Polska Samodzielna Brygada Spadochronowa

Reports

Allied HQ Reports	September 1944
BBC-London	September 1944
OKW-Berichte	September 1944
The Times, London	September 1944
Eyewitness accounts	

Photographs

Bundesarchiv, Koblenz (150)
Imperial War Museum, London (45)
Sikorski Institute, London (20)
Gemeentearchief Arnhem (10)
Ir. J. Voskuil, Oosterbeek (10)
Archiv J. Piekalkiewicz

Foreword

'The gallant defeat': The bitter fighting at Arnhem which ended with the defeat of the gallant British 1st Airborne Division brought the Germans their last victory of the war. It began with Montgomery's conviction that a single thrust into Germany, towards the capital of the Third Reich, would finish the war. It ended in darkness and fog on the night of 26 September 1944 with the élite British troops, earmarked for 'Objective Berlin', withdrawing across the Lower Rhine. Operation 'Market Garden' was, in the words of an English historian, 'the greatest airborne enterprise of World War II, but it was also the most extraordinary one.' Because of the insatiable ambitions of individual Allied military commanders, the Allied airborne army — a modern winged cavalry, intended for employment only in decisive battles or for special tasks— was nonchalantly sacrificed.

The beginnings of this ill-starred venture can be traced back to the headquarters of the 1st Airborne Army at Ascot, near London, some days before the operation was actually launched. And the first in what was to be a series of short-comings may be attributed to British Intelligence, whose assessment of the enemy situation was usually so reliable. In this instance, however, a realistic picture of what was happening in the area where it was proposed to stage Operation 'Market Garden' was never forthcoming. Dutch military experts were excluded from the planning and preparations for the operation, and by so doing the planners burnt their fingers. The operation was to be fought on Dutch soil, and the Dutch experts serving with the Allies were the only ones really familiar with their country's tricky environment. Moreover they were especially well-informed as to the feasibility and hazards associated with armoured warfare in their homeland. However, those responsible for planning the operation were not prepared to listen to any advice or recital of facts which did not fit in with their own preconceived ideas. Among other things they ignored warnings concerning the presence of German Panzer units in or near the proposed dropping zones with the result that many of the Allied paratroops were shot before they reached the ground or mowed down shortly after landing in the flat open terrain. Of those who survived the initial ordeal many suffocated in the cellars of burning houses in Arnhem during nine days of fighting from house to house, room to room and cellar to cellar. Of the 10,095 men who dropped in the lower Rhine region, no less than 7,872 were killed, wounded or captured.

On the German side the Waffen SS (according to the historian Erich Kern, the SS chronicler) fought their most chivalrous battle. Men wearing the *Totenkopf* (Death's Head) badge had destroyed and devastated whole districts of Warsaw during the uprising there, but at Arnhem medical orderlies of the Hohenstaufen and Frundsberg divisions saved the lives of 2,200 British casualties, and handed out chocolate, biscuits and tobacco. Even the wounded, with groups of men who fought on and refused to surrender despite the hopelessness of their position, were supplied with bandages. These humanitarian measures were due largely to the initiative of the divisional medical officer

Dr Skalka — whose samaritan services were subsequently rewarded by the British with two years in a prisoner of war camp.

The battle for Arnhem had one sequel that is rarely mentioned: the Allied defeat at Arnhem gave Hitler's self-confidence a boost. This led him to prepare Operation *'Wacht am Rhein'*— the Ardennes Offensive — a gamble which was launched in December 1944 and which ended ultimately in disaster.

Janusz Piekalkiewicz

Dramatis Personae

Barlow, H. N., Colonel, Deputy to Brigadier Hicks

Bittrich, Wilhelm, Obergruppenführer, Commanding II. SS Panzer Korps

Bradley, Omar, General (US), Commanding 12th US Army Group

Brereton, Lewis H., Lt General (US), Commanding 1st Allied Airborne Army

Browning, F. A. M., Lt General, Commanding 1st Allied Airborne Corps, Deputy to Gen Brereton

Christiansen, Friedrich, General, Air Force, Army C-in-C Netherlands

Dempsey, Sir Miles C., Lt General, Commanding 2nd British Army

Dobie, D., Lt Colonel, Commanding 1st Parachute Battalion

Eisenhower, Dwight D., General (US), C-in-C Allied Forces in Western Europe

Fitch, J. A., Lt Colonel, Commanding 3rd Parachute Battalion

Frost, John D., Lt Colonel, Commanding 2nd Parachute Battalion

Gavin, James M., Maj General (US), Commanding 82nd Airborne Division

Gräbner, Kurt, Hauptsturmführer, Commanding Reconnaissance Unit of the 9th SS Panzer Div

Hackett, John W., Brigadier, Commanding 4th Parachute Brigade

Harmel, Heinz, Brigadeführer, Commanding 10th SS Panzer Division Frundsberg

Harzer, Walter, Obersturmbannführer, Commanding 9th SS Panzer Division Hohenstaufen

Hicks, Philip H., Brigadier, Commanding 1st Airlanding Brigade

Horrocks, Sir Brian, Lt General, Commanding XXX Armoured and Infantry Corps of General Dempsey's Army

Krafft, Sepp, Sturmbannführer, Commanding SS Panzergrenadier Training and Reserve Bn 16

Lathbury, Gerald W., Brigadier, Commanding 1st Parachute Brigade

Lea, G. H., Lt Colonel, Commanding 11th Parachute Battalion

McCardie, W. D. H., Lt Colonel, Commanding 2nd South Staffordshire Bn

Model, Walter, Field Marshal, Commander in Chief Army Group B

Montgomery, Sir Bernard, Field Marshal, Commanding 21st British Army Group

Patton, George S. jun., General (US), Commanding 3rd US Army

Runstedt, Gerd v., General Field Marshal, Commander in Chief West

Sosabowski, Stanislaw, Major General, Commanding 1st Polish Independent Parachute Brigade

Student, Kurt, Colonel General, Commander-in-Chief 1st Parachute Army

Taylor, Maxwell D., Major General (US), Commanding 101st Airborne Division

Tempelhof, Hans-Georg v., Colonel of General Staff of Army Group B

Urquhart, Robert E., Major General, Commanding 1st Airborne Divison

Zangen, Gustav v., General of Infantry, Commander in Chief 15th Army

Zwolanski, Ludwik, Captain, Liaison Officer of 1st Polish Independent Parachute Brigade with HQ 1st Airborne Division

Prologue

In summer 1944 the German armies were retreating on all fronts. Over a million American and British soldiers had broken out of their Normandy beachheads, captured Paris and linked up in the Vosges with General Patch's army advancing from the Mediterranean. In the north the British 21st Army Group, comprising the 2nd British and 1st Canadian Armies, had over-run almost the whole of Belgium and in several places had reached the Dutch border. But now the British advance faltered.

At this time the Allies were convinced they had a clear picture of the German situation. The combined Allied Intelligence Committee reported that 'no organised resistance may be expected after 1 December 1944; indeed it may well end before that date'. SHAEF, the Supreme HQ Allied Expeditionary Force, was of the same opinion.

At the beginning of September it was being said that the German Army was no longer a coherent force, that its units were scattered and disorganised, and its demoralised troops short of arms and equipment. At the War Office in London, General John Kennedy, the Director of Operations, wrote on 6 September: 'If we continue to advance at the same pace as that of recent weeks we should be in Berlin on 28 September'.

So, with victory seemingly in sight, Field Marshal Bernard L. Montgomery drafted a plan that was designed to administer the coup de grace. His tanks were to push forward into Holland, cross the Rhine at Arnhem, thrust southwards into the Ruhr and hopefully, march into Berlin with the conquering Field Marshal at their head. In his Operational Appreciation M 525, dated 14 September 1944, Montgomery summarised his plan:

'(1) Since the fall of Le Havre our supply situation has improved, and we are now in a position to undertake operations to capture the Ruhr.

(2) Although the port of Antwerp is now in our hands we cannot use it because the enemy commands the north of the Scheldt. Clearing the Scheldt estuary will be the main task of the 1st Canadian Army.

(3) The US 1st Army has crossed the German border on our right flank and has reached the Siegfried Line. Further south the US 3rd Army has established a bridgehead over the Moselle.

(4) In conjunction with the 12th Army Group we now wish to concentrate on operations to encircle, isolate and occupy the industrial heart of Germany. Our immediate aim is the Ruhr but in the course of the proposed operations we propose to open up Antwerp and Rotterdam. Once these deep water ports are functioning our maintenance facilities will improve and operations can develop. Occupation of the Ruhr will follow; this will open the way to a powerful thrust deep into Germany by way of the northern route.

(5) My intention, therefore is the destruction of all enemy forces west of the line Zwolle - Deventer — Kleve — Venlo—Maastricht, to advance east and to encircle the Ruhr.

(6) Operational boundaries will be as follows:
Inclusive to the 12th Army Group: Hasselt—Sithard—Garzweiler—Leverkusen-on-Rhine.
Inclusive to 21 Army Group: Opladen-Warburg-Braunschweig.

(7) D Day for the operation is Sunday 17 September but if bad weather hinders airborne operations on that day it is possible that there may be a postponement.'

In Montgomery's headquarters at Laaken near Brussels the proposed operation was acclaimed as imaginative and audacious. Montgomery himself radiated confidence: 'One bold thrust will take us to Berlin, and the war can be finished by Christmas.'

The main problem was that the terrain between the Belgian border and Arnhem was swampy and criss-crossed by numerous canals; there was only one road and the rest of the countryside was totally unsuitable for an advance by armour. Nor could such an advance commence until the British XXX Corps were certain that the bridges across the successive river lines of Maas, Waal and Rhine could be used. At first three, then subsequently four airborne divisions were earmarked for a surprise assault to capture these vital bridges.

The principal objective of Operation 'Market Garden' was the massive steel and concrete road bridge over the lower Rhine at Arnhem; a nearby pontoon bridge and a twin-track railway bridge some 4km west of the town downstream were secondary objectives. The capture of these bridges was to be undertaken by the British 1st Airborne Division under the command of Major General R. E. Urquhart.

Speaking after the operation General Bradley said: 'When I first heard of it I was flabbergasted; I could not have been more astonished if I had seen Montgomery the teetotaller suffering from a hangover.' The American General Lewis H. Brereton, the commander of the First Allied Airborne Army — a distinguished officer who had done well with the (US) tactical air force, but who had never previously commanded airborne troops — was to be responsible for the execution of Operation 'Market Garden'.

Staff officers at Montgomery's headquarters were persuaded that XXX Corps (Lieut General B. G. Horrocks) could smash through the thin crust of the German defence line in the initial assault. Once this line had been penetrated they considered that the Germans had insufficient reserves to stop the British armour before it reached the Zuider Zee. In fact, their general opinion was that the Germans no longer posed a threat to the Allied forces.

General Browning summed up the essential features of the plan this way: 'We will lay down an airborne carpet, over which our ground troops will drive to turn the northern flank of the Siegfried Line.' The operation as a whole was code-named 'Market Garden' but it was to be in two parts. In Operation 'Market' Browning's airborne troops would be dropped to provide the 'carpet' across which General Horrock's tanks would roll into Holland from Belgium in the 'Garden' part of the operation.

Brereton wanted to use some 35,000 men in 'Market Garden' — almost twice the number of airborne troops used in the Normandy invasion. Moreover, he believed that if the element of surprise was to be exploited to the full, then the three and a half divisions which were to be committed would have to be dropped almost simultaneously. In the event there were not enough aircraft and gliders to carry this number of men and their equipment in a single lift. Consequently only half the troops and a minimum of heavy equipment — guns, jeeps etc — could be dropped or landed on the first day.

Compared with 'Market', previous airborne operations had been small fry. But all of them had one feature in common: months of careful planning had preceded their execution. Yet on this occasion Montgomery allowed Brereton and his staff a mere seven days in which to draw up and finalise the arrangements for what was to be the biggest airborne operation of the war.

Meanwhile, the Germans were taking full advantage of the unexpected pause in the war. On 2 July 1944 Hitler had sacked the able and experienced Field Marshal von Runstedt. Just over two months later, on 4 September 1944, however, von Rundstedt was recalled and appointed Commander-in-Chief France and North-West Europe. Under his direction the haphazard German withdrawals were countermanded. About this time too General Student established the headquarters for his recently created First Airborne Army near Vugh, and the II SS-Panzer Korps under SS-Obergruppenführer (General) Willi Bittrich was concentrating around Arnhem. Moreover, in the Hotel Tafelberg, nestling in a lovely park in the Oosterbeek suburb of Arnhem, Field Marshal Model had installed the headquarters of his Army Group B.

The II SS-Panzer Korps, consisting of the 9th and 10th SS-Panzer Divisions, had suffered heavy losses, but the Korps remained an experienced and élite formation, the morale of which was extremely high. After the battle General Bittrich used the expression 'the courage of desperation' to describe the bearing of his men.

The 9th SS-Panzer Division Hohenstaufen, under the command of W. Harzer, had concentrated in a wooded nature reserve north-east of Arnhem, where its tanks were easily concealed. The units of the 10th SS-Panzer Division, Frundsberg, commanded by H. Harmel, were drawn up in a semi-circle starting in the north-east and finishing in the south-east outskirts of Arnhem. Instead of their usual quota of about 9,000 men, the Hohenstaufen Division had less than 6,000, while the Frundsberg had only 3,500. Obersturmbannführer (Lt Col) Harzer had some twenty Panther tanks at his disposal, but several were unfit for action. However he had a considerable number of armoured vehicles equipped with heavy machine guns, assault guns, light armoured troop carriers and personnel carriers. Harmel had practically no tanks and only a very few other armoured vehicles. But both SS divisions could put up almost their full complement of artillery, including mortars and anti-aircraft guns.

Allied air reconnaissance had failed to discover that Field Marshal Model's headquarters had been located at Oosterbeek near the proposed dropping zone of the

British 1st Airborne Division. On the other hand, though Model was one of Hitler's most percipient strategists, neither he nor any of his staff were expecting an Allied airborne attack anywhere near Oosterbeek. They could not believe Montgomery would ever undertake such a foolhardy enterprise.

Information concerning the enemy's disposition is one of the most important pre-requisites for the success of any operation. 'Market Garden' was no exception. Allied agents operating in Holland and members of the Dutch Resistance had gathered a good deal of intelligence. But nearly all of these sources of information were amateur with little military training, and consequently unable to identify the hotch-potch of German units by their uniforms or to distinguish between types in the jumble of tanks and guns which were flooding into the area. Only an expert could have sifted such evidence accurately, and even he would have found the job doubly difficult because of the disorganisation prevalent in Wehrmacht units in the summer of 1944. In the event the data as received was extremely confusing: for example, some formations sometimes designated as divisions were actually of less than regimental strength.

If it was difficult enough to procure information at this time, getting it back to London was even more hazardous. Operating a radio transmitter was dicing with death, for German detector radio location cars were operating round the clock. The Allied Intelligence Service, of course, gleaned other information from prisoners of war and by means of aerial reconnaissance. In the final analysis, the accuracy of the conclusions drawn from all the available data depended largely on the ability of those charged with assembling the total intelligence picture.

After the battle General Urquhart recalled that 'such information as actually got through to us was of very little use in the planning stage of the operation. I knew very little about what went on in and around Arnhem despite the fact that my intelligence staff followed up every scrap of information. But I knew that news received from the Continent was probably out of date anyway if only because it had already been passed from one headquarters to another — from the 2nd Army to our Airborne Army. In any case such things were exclusively Army matters and we had to content ourselves with this fact. Browning himself told me that we would probably meet only insignificant German forces with a few tanks.'

An element of the Dutch Resistance did get a message through to Britain warning that German Panzer units had moved into Holland, apparently for refurbishing and refitting. According to another message 'from an unknown source' reporting to the Intelligence Section of the British 2nd Army, the main concentration areas of the Panzer units were Eindhoven and Nijmegen. A few days prior to the launching of Operation 'Market Garden' British Intelligence at SHAEF concluded that the units concerned were the 9th and probably the 10th SS-Panzer Divisions being re-equipped from a tank

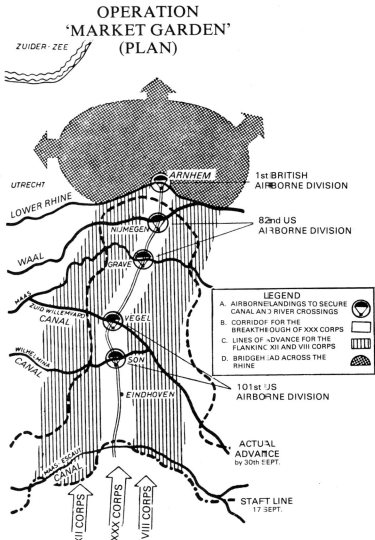

OPERATION 'MARKET GARDEN' (PLAN)

ZUIDER·ZEE

UTRECHT

LOWER RHINE

ARNHEM — 1st BRITISH AIRBORNE DIVISION

NIJMEGEN — 82nd US AIRBORNE DIVISION

WAAL

GRAVE

MAAS

ZUID WILLEMVAARD CANAL

VEGEL

WILHELMINA CANAL

SON — 101st US AIRBORNE DIVISION

EINDHOVEN

MAAS-ESCAUT CANAL

XII CORPS

XXX CORPS

VIII CORPS

ACTUAL ADVANCE by 30th SEPT.

STAR T LINE 17 SEPT.

LEGEND
A. AIRBORNE LANDINGS TO SECURE CANAL AND RIVER CROSSINGS
B. CORRIDOR FOR THE BREAKTHROUGH OF XXX CORPS
C. LINES OF ADVANCE FOR THE FLANKING XII AND VIII CORPS
D. BRIDGEHEAD ACROSS THE RHINE

depot near Kleve, a few miles from Arnhem on the German side of the border. But the Intelligence Staff of Montgomery's 21st Army Group disagreed and discounted any idea of SS-Panzer divisions in the area; On 16 September an Intelligence officer at the HQ of General Dempsey's British 2nd Army also deduced correctly that the units of II SS-Panzer Korps which escaped annihilation in Normandy had been moved to the Arnhem area, but the rest of the Intelligence staff at 2nd Army HQ were sceptical; no confirmation was forthcoming from Dutch Resistance sources and there was no evidence of tanks in aerial photographs of the region.

Three days previously, on 13 September (ie four days before the launching of Operation 'Market Garden'), XXX Corps HQ declared that '. . the latest reconnaissance reports indicate that there are only a few infantry formations in reserve in Holland, and no more than 50 to 100 tanks.'

On 15 September the Intelligence Information Department at the War Office noted that the SS-Panzer Division was Hohenstaufen deployed along the Ijssel River. 'Units of this division are reported to have been seen at Arnhem and as far away as Zutphen-Apeldoorn. HQ probably in Eefde. Defences being constructed along the Ijssel.'

In fact the headquarters of Harzer's 9th SS-Panzer Division Hohenstaufen was in Beekbergen, that of Harmel's 10th SS-Panzer Division Frundsberg in Ruurlo and the headquarters of Bittrich's II SS-Panzer Korps at Doetinchem. The whole of the Hohenstaufen Division had now been deployed on the west bank of the Ijssel.

On 15 September the 'Kees' Group — the signal section of the Arnhem Resistance organisation — transmitted this message to London: 'The concentration area of the Hohenstaufen Division is near Arnhem. This is the assembly area for units of the SS Division which we have already reported. A "Harzer HQ" is said to be located in Arnhem itself; this is probably a detachment of a formation deployed south of Arnhem'.

Not even the German Commander-in-Chief, Field Marshal von Rundstedt, knew the actual strength of German troops under his command in the Eindhoven-Arnhem region. For example, he was unaware that the 9th SS-Panzer Division Hohenstaufen (Harzer) had been ordered to transfer its operational vehicles to the 10th SS-Panzer Division (Harmel), which was reforming east of the Ijssel, and that Harzer — who had no intention of weakening his division still further — was conspiring to thwart the transfer. Harzer had ordered the tracks to be stripped from his armoured vehicles at Arnhem and had some of the guns dismantled. He then informed Bittrich's Korps HQ that these vehicles were non-operational. They were soon to be a decisive factor in the battle for Arnhem.

Meanwhile the Allies were unwittingly making their own contribution to their forthcoming defeat. On the afternoon of Wednesday, 13 September the SS-Panzer Division Hohenstaufen started to evacuate the Arnhem area. Under normal conditions this move would have been completed by Saturday, 16 September at the latest, and some of the strongest units in the area would have cleared the 1st Airborne Division's dropping zone. However, attacks by Allied fighter bombers on railway traffic from 13 September onwards and the blowing up of railway installations by the Dutch Resistance combined to delay the move of the Hohenstaufen. In consequence some of its units were still in the Veluwe area on 17 September, nicely in position to confront the British airborne force.

The dropping zones selected were stretches of lush green pastureland, interspersed with villages and farmsteads. The one west of Arnhem was demarcated by the Arnhem-Ede-Utrecht road and railway, the Arnhem-Wageringen and Arnhem-Oosterbeek roads, and the Rhine. The whole area, apart from the low-lying land near the river to the west of Oosterbeek, was well wooded, but in the vicinity of Arnhem's suburbs the trees

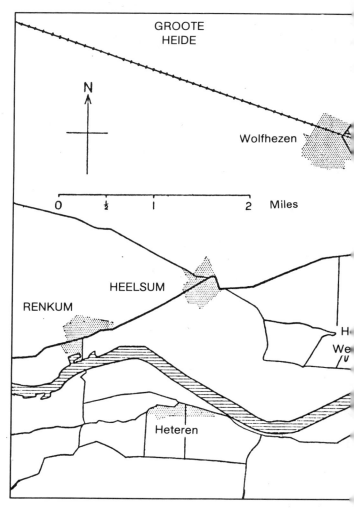

thinned out and the terrain took on the character of a country house's parkland. This sort of country was ill-suited to quick concentration of an airborne force because it offered few open tracts of ground for landings. Equally, though, it hampered the movement of enemy vehicles. Although roads fanned out from the dropping zones to encourage hope of a quick advance into the town, there was another hazard: the area surrounding Arnhem and Nijmegen, between the Rhine and the Waal, was a marsh intersected by numerous canals and drainage ditches. The soft wet soil would seriously handicap deployment of heavy equipment; vehicles could not be driven off the few roads which had been constructed on the embankments of the dikes; while for tanks the terrain was to prove quite impossible.

Only one of the senior Allied commanders had serious misgivings about Operation 'Market Garden.' He was General Sosabowski, commander of the Polish 1st Independent Parachute Brigade. Unfortunately his views carried little weight among his colleagues in the Allied HQ and he was not taken seriously. To Sosabowski, Operation 'Comet' — one of several subsidiary operations scheduled to precede 'Market Garden' —

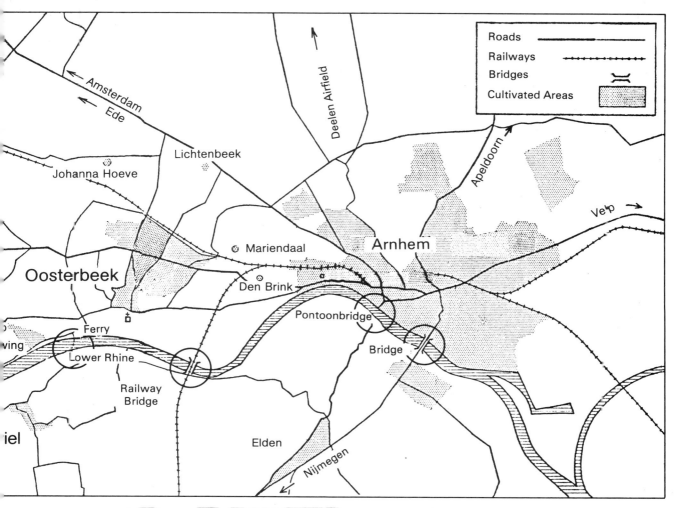

looked particularly ill-advised and he protested strongly to Generals Urquhart and Browning. He insisted the he must have written orders spelling out his role in what he was convinced would be a suicidal operation; he had no intention of being held responsible for its consequences. Sosabowski was certain that the British had not only underestimated the strength of German forces in the area but had also failed to grasp the significance and importance of Arnhem to the Germans. He was convinced that the German High Command regarded Arnhem as a gate leading straight into the German Fatherland; it was inconceivable to him that the Germans would leave the gate open. That Sosabowski's speculations were correct the British were to discover later from a captured German document which bluntly stated that 'the High Command considers that the battle at Arnhem will decide the fate of the German people'.

Sosabowski found the theory that the Germans had left only a few inferior troops and decrepit tanks to

Left: *Field Marshal Montgomery* (centre) *with a Belgian Resistance fighter.*

13

defend Arnhem quite incredible. He was strongly critical, too, of the British intention to drop the 1st Airborne Division 10km from their objective, which would mean a march to the bridge that could take up to five hours. 'Where is the surprise then?' he asked. 'Even the most stupid Germans will guess our objective.' But his superiors were unmoved. Above all, Sosabowski was concerned to know what he was supposed to do if the Arnhem bridge was not in British hands when his brigade was dropped into Holland. According to the operational plan, his men were to be be dropped on the *southern* bank of the Rhine, while their artillery and other heavy equipment were to be landed *north* of the river. To his utter consternation Sosabowski learned that he and his men were expected to take the bridge from the Germans if the British assault failed.

For the British 1st Airborne Division it was now vital to know what is in store for them north of the Rhine.

Urquhart said later that he 'would have preferred' his troops to have been dropped 'on both sides of the Rhine as close to the road bridge as possible'. But the RAF would not have this. According to bomber crews returning from missions over this area anti-aircraft fire around the bridge was extremely heavy. Furthermore, after dropping off their gliders the towing aircraft would have to turn and fly over Deelen airfield, seven miles north of Arnhem, and thus, it was said, would be exposed to heavy AA fire from guns around the airfield. Furthermore, Intelligence experts maintained that the low-lying polder land south of the bridge was totally unsuitable for gliders and paratroops. Only later did it emerge that there were neither AA guns nor fighter aircraft at Deelen. According to Harzer, the day before Operation 'Market Garden' was launched the garrison at Deelen consisted of a mere handful of Luftwaffe ground staff, plus four 20mm guns and a couple of 88mm AA guns from the Hohenstaufen Division. The conclusion that it was impossible to use the polder land for landing gliders or as a dropping zone proved equally correct.

During any airborne operation the pilot of an aircraft remains in command until the troops leave his plane. In this instance the RAF insisted on having the last word in the choice of landing and dropping zones. In his report on the operations Urquhart wrote subsequently: 'Not only the Army, but the RAF also were too pessimistic in their assessment of the AA guns'. Because of this the landing and dropping zones selected were several miles too far from the objectives.

Just 24 hours before the launching of Operation 'Market Garden' the airborne troops got another hint of what to expect when they touched down in Holland. Returning from a mission over The Hague Allied fighter aircraft fitted with cameras took photographs over Arnhem. When these were developed they showed clear evidence of tanks. However, when Urquhart showed the pictures to General Browning the latter is reputed to have reassured him: 'I wouldn't worry your head about it: those things are probably stuck'!

The German High Command was fully conscious of

Air Reconnaissance Photographs 10.9.1944.
Above left: *The ferry from Driel to Heveadorp.*
Above right: *The prime objective: the bridge at Arnhem.*
Below right: *The railway bridge.*

the threat posed by a large-scale airborne operation. In fact, back in 1943, as a precautionary measure, the Commander-in-Chief of the Luftwaffe had issued secret instructions regarding the action to be taken in the event of an Allied airborne assault:

Defence against Parachute and Air-Landing Troops in the event of an Airborne Assault
Conduct of the Battle
(1) Airborne troops constitute a more versatile menace than normal ground troops. They can exploit the factors of surprise and deception more easily and they have more opportunities to employ ruses. The defence can be surprised time and again and repeatedly face totally unexpected situations.
(2) For this reason the defence must take an imaginative view of the possibilities open to enemy airborne troops and plan accordingly. One important relevant factor which can be decisive stems from the fact that the defenders may well be stronger than the attackers at the beginning of an operation and they should exploit this fact by acting quickly.
(3) Methods of attack which may be expected:
(a) Speedy (ie a surprise onslaught) — when the enemy airborne force is dropped directly on the objective.
(b) Deliberate — when an assault force is dropped or landed in close proximity to the objective but beyond the range of the defenders' weapons; it rallies, approaches and then attacks.
The enemy will undoubtedly launch surprise airborne

assaults to seize or destroy important objectives and to create havoc behind our lines. (This type of operation is a speciality of the British). Small detachments of specialist parachutists can also be dropped some time before a major assault. Such men will have been allotted special tasks and they may remain in hiding for some time until they can work their way up to their objectives.

The indications are that Anglo-Saxon airborne troops tend to favour the deliberate method. This has definite benefits so far as the defence is concerned because surprise — the airborne attackers' main advantage — is less easy to achieve and time is on the side of the defence.

(4) Airborne assaults will generally be preceded by an aerial bombardment and the first paratroops will be dropped immediately afterwards. However in the hope of achieving complete surprise the air attacks may be dispensed with; alternatively other targets may be bombed as feint to distract the defence.

(5) Anglo-American paratroops are well trained in the techniques associated with dropping at night, and it is known that they practise night operations. Thus special vigilance is needed during the hours of darkness.

(6) Well-trained paratroops can be ready for action within a few seconds of reaching the ground.

15

Terrain

(7) Airborne troops can be set down on almost any kind of terrain nowadays. Landings on stony or rocky ground (as happened at Narvik) in bush-country, in plantations and on fruit farms (as on Crete) and in an area criss-crossed with waterways (such as Holland) are perfectly feasible.

The only impossible landing areas are those where there are high tension electric cables, densely populated regions, ravines, precipices and thick forest.

Extensive, relatively empty regions are needed for large-scale airborne operations. Large formations could not be landed in many parts of the Brittany peninsula, for instance, because of the large number of single high trees and restricted stretches of open country. But small airborne units can still operate in such country.

(8) Gliders are more dependent on terrain than paratroops. Nevertheless they can land in relatively small spaces.

(9) There is no terrain which can be classed as absolutely proof against an airborne attack by paratroops or glider-borne infantry.

Vital ground must therefore be classified and defined as:
(a) Terrain vulnerable to airborne assault (ie suited to the dropping of large formations of paratroops or the landing of gliders).
(b) Terrain where transport aircraft could land (ie additional to (a) above, where landing strips could be constructed).

(10) The approximate size of a parachute battalion dropping zone is 800 x 300m.

(11) The landing and unloading of a battalion airlifted in transport planes to a medium-sized airfield can be completed in 45 minutes provided there is no enemy opposition. More time is needed to unload artillery and other heavy equipment. The Anglo-American airborne forces have a large number of modern American transport aircraft. Consequently if and when Anglo-American formations are employed operationally we can expect them to use planes each of which will carry 40 to 60 fully-equipped men.

Gliders

(12) Gliders are not restricted to airfields; they can land in any open space.

Small gliders are capable of performing simple aerobatics and by diving can quickly penetrate a curtain of AA fire; they are also capable of surmounting obstacles in their glide path. Most gliders are equipped with machine-guns and thus are capable of returning the fire of the defenders. They may be used at night but only when the night is light (ie several nights before and after a full moon). In night operations, however, only area landings — as distinct from 'target' landings — are possible.

(13) The enemy possess a large number of gliders and is constantly adding to them.

English types are:

Horsa, with two pilots and 28 men or a 3-ton payload.

Hamilcar, with 50 to 60 men or a 6-ton payload.

Hengist — possibly a smaller type than the Hamilcar.

American types are:

Waco C-G-3 which can carry nine men,

Waco C-G-4 which can carry 15 men or a light vehicle and its crew.

(14) English gliders can be used — according to their load capacity and the known training methods — to carry, apart from troops, heavy weapons and heavy equipment, on to the battlefield.

However, the possibility of single assaults by gliders (two Horsa gliders were employed at Drontheim) cannot be dismissed.

(15) Every British paratrooper has at least two years' service — as an infantryman, gunner or engineer — before he becomes a parachutist. Each parachute company has a company commander and four officers.

(16) The British paratrooper spends a lot of time on jumping training and he is capable of dropping, with his weapons, from heights of only 60m.

(17) British paratroops are armed with rifles, machine-pistols, machine-guns (but not heavy machine-guns) medium, light and heavy mortars. They have few heavy weapons.

(18) The glider-borne troops are similarly equipped, but also have flamethrowers, heavy machine-guns, anti-tank guns, light AA guns and portable 7.5mm howitzers. Armoured machine-gun carriers and small armoured patrol-cars can be air-lifted.

American Airborne Troops

(19) Like the British the US Airborne Force is exclusively manned by volunteers. A strict selection for physical and intellectual ability and a hard training make it an élite corps.

(20) American paratroops are armed with heavier weapons than their British counterpart. They have pistols, semi-automatic Garand-rifles, light machine-guns, light and heavy mortars, as well as heavy machine-guns and parachute artillery (possibly 7.5cm portable mountain howitzers).

(21) It is said that the American airborne forces are also equipped with 2cm and 3.7cm AA/anti-tank guns and with 10.5cm howitzers.

Defence Methods

(22) (a) Potential landing and dropping zones in areas vulnerable to an airborne assault should be blocked.
(b) Barriers should be erected in front and around defence installations and defensive localities.
(c) Mines and wire are particularly useful in defence against airborne troops. Minefields are the most dreaded of the silent enemies of airborne forces, and areas where the enemy believes mines have been planted are avoided. Therefore the maximum use should be made of mines. Low density or dummy minefields have to be dealt with in the same way as proper minefields, and thus constitute a deterrent. Dummy minefields are especially useful where there is the threat of an airborne

A jeep is loaded into a Horsa MkII.

attack. Like the attacker the defender needs to employ every ruse at his disposal.

(d) Stakes, ditches, earth banks, heaps of stones or manure, piles of wood and planks, old immobile carts and wagons are additional ways of blocking landing zones.

(23) Defence installations must always be capable of all-round fire.

Guns (artillery) often warrant special attention by airborne troops and it is therefore essential that battery and troop positions should be sited with all-round defence in mind, and with enough machine guns properly deployed.

Vehicles constitute particularly vulnerable booty to enemy airborne troops.

Vehicles should not therefore be left in areas that are patently insecure, but concentrated where they can be looked after.

(24) Observation posts sited on suitably elevated buildings etc, such as church spires, have an important role to play, especially in thinly-populated areas. If the descent of paratroops is spotted and reported early on, the chances of defeating an airborne assault are greatly increased.

(25) Communication Links.

In an airborne attack exposed telephone cables are liable to be destroyed.

Warning systems must therefore be organised in all important defence installations.

A good communications system is vital in the fog of war which is bound to be created during an airborne assault.

(26) Mobile Reserve at Instant Readiness.

In general even the smallest units should allocate vehicles to their mobile reserve. These vehicles should be equipped with machine-guns, anti-tank or 2cm AA guns or improvised mountings, so that it is possible to shoot from the vehicle. Machine-pistols, hand grenades and portable searchlights (if possible) should be kept ready for immediate use. If available an AA section should be earmarked for deployment with the reserve. Finally it must be remembered that tanks and armoured cars are the airborne troops' most dangerous adversaries.

(27) Defensive Methods

The defence must be aggressive. Therefore the forces available must not be dispersed, although sizeable reserves must be held in readiness. If precise information is not forthcoming from observation posts and reconnaissance patrols then what appears to be the most threatening enemy party must be promptly attacked in order to destroy the first waves of paratroops before they can concentrate into a coherent force. Even minor forces have prospects of success in the initial phases of an assault. Delay and hesitation are fatal; to the paratroops every minute counts towards the development of their fighting power. Nevertheless a certain amount of caution is called for in the initial stages in regard to the deployment of reserves. It is essential that vital points and installations are properly guarded even while

A motorcycle and side-car in a Horsa Mk II.

offensive action is in progress. The important thing is to diagnose the enemy's intentions and not to be misled by a ruse (eg feint attacks, or the dropping of a diversionary group of paratroops).

(28) Opening fire.

The chances of hitting paratroops during their descent are low; shooting at short and medium range is more likely to be successful. Paratroops are most vulnerable during the few minutes after touching the ground, unhooking their parachutes and assembling, and if the assembly area is not under direct observation, the use of indirect fire (particularly by machine guns in enfilade) should be considered.

Conclusion

It must be assumed that Anglo-American airborne formations will continue to expand and that they will be employed in airborne operations on a far greater scale than hitherto — possibly in massive operations far behind our coast defences and fronts, in order to gain some strategic or tactical advantage. All counter-measures therefore must be constantly reviewed and kept up to date.

(Extract from: Secret Memorandum 10/22. Issued in July 1943)

The following summary of the operational instructions — Pilots' Notes for Horsa I Glider — issued to glider pilots by the RAF gives insight into some of the many problems underlying Operation 'Market Garden'.

Part I: Controls and equipment for pilots

(1) *Introductory:* The Horsa I is a high-wing, monoplane glider designed for transporting 25 troops with their equipment or military equipment and light vehicles.

The main wheels of the tricycle undercarriage are jettisonable, and a landing skid protects the fuselage when making belly landings. Benches are fitted in the main cabin for the troops, and eight military equipment containers (with parachutes) are slung in cells, four on each side, under the wing. The pilot's cockpit in the nose seats two pilots side by side...

Lighting, Radio & Signalling Equipment

(27) *Radio:* There is a T.R.9D set installed with a remote control unit (4) for the pilots mounted on the left of starboard pilot's seat. The head-set jack socket for the port pilot is secured to the seat frame outboard of the seat.

(28) *Intercommunication:* The T.R.9D set provides intercommunication between the glider and tug pilots...

Part II: Handling and Flying Notes for Pilots

(1) *Introduction:* (i) These notes are for the guidance of pilots flying Horsa glider combinations. Tug aircraft pilots should also refer to Part III and the appropriate appendix thereto covering the tug aircraft used. (ii) The method of signalling (intercom or visual) to be used between the glider and tug pilots, both on the ground and in the air, should be agreed and the code of visual signals to be used in emergency (or if intercom is not to be used) should be in accordance with the instructions laid down by the Command concerned. *Note:* It is of vital importance that glider and tug pilots shall agree and understand the code of signals to be used. The tug PILOT is CAPTAIN of the COMBINATION...

(4) *Fitness of Aircraft for Flight:* Ensure that the total weight and C.G. position are within the permitted limits. Heavy loads should in no case be carried without calculating the C.G. position by means of the loading charts.

Rough guides to loading are: (a) Two pilots, or a first pilot and ballast in the second pilot's place, should be carried. *Note:* Gliders must not be flown light without a second pilot or ballast in lieu. (b) Any load should be disposed evenly about a point one third of the chord length aft of the leading edge at the wing root...

(7) *Take-off:* (i) Keep directly behind the tug. (ii) At an ample margin above stalling speed (see para. 14) pull off gently and hold near the ground until tug takes-off. (iii) When the tug is clear of the ground, climb gently, to maintain a 'high tow' position (as defined in Para. 10). (iv) If the Mk II indicator is to be used, allowing three minutes after take-off for the gyro to erect, zero the pointer; this should be done with the tug flying straight and the glider central below the slip-stream (the instrument only functions in the low tow position).

(10) *Best Position on Tow:* To obtain the maximum rate of climb and range it is of importance that, once steady climbing conditions have been reached and in level flight, the glider shall maintain the correct position in relation to the tug flight path. Recommended positions are as follows: (i) *High Tow Position:* Directly behind the tug and one half the wing span of the tug above it (with experience this position may be gauged by observing the

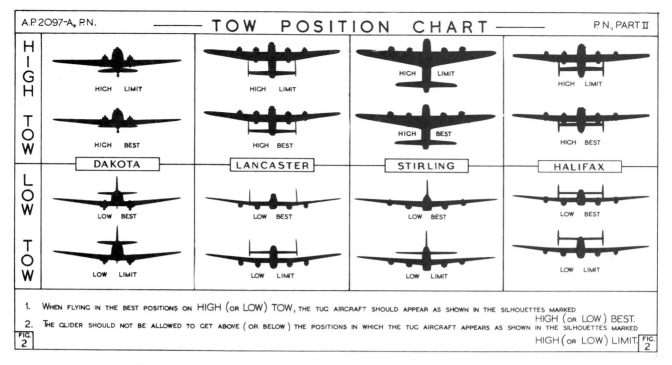

	HIGH TOW			
	HIGH LIMIT	HIGH LIMIT	HIGH LIMIT	HIGH LIMIT
	HIGH BEST	HIGH BEST	HIGH BEST	HIGH BEST
	DAKOTA	LANCASTER	STIRLING	HALIFAX
LOW TOW	LOW BEST	LOW BEST	LOW BEST	LOW BEST
	LOW LIMIT	LOW LIMIT	LOW LIMIT	LOW LIMIT

1. WHEN FLYING IN THE BEST POSITIONS ON HIGH (OR LOW) TOW, THE TUG AIRCRAFT SHOULD APPEAR AS SHOWN IN THE SILHOUETTES MARKED HIGH (OR LOW) BEST.
2. THE GLIDER SHOULD NOT BE ALLOWED TO GET ABOVE (OR BELOW) THE POSITIONS IN WHICH THE TUG AIRCRAFT APPEARS AS SHOWN IN THE SILHOUETTES MARKED HIGH (OR LOW) LIMIT.

FIG. 2   FIG. 2

Above: *Instructions for the best towing position.*
Right: *A container is fastened under the wing of a Dakota.*

relationship between the tug tailplane and mainplane) it is not sufficient to keep just clear of the slipstream. (ii) *Low Tow Position:* Directly behind the tug and one half the wing span of the tug *below* it. This position is to be preferred, except during initial climb, for the following reasons: (a) The glider tends to maintain position more naturally than in the high tow position. (b) The correct vertical position is such that the glider is just clear of the slipstream and can therefore be more precisely gauged. *Note:* (i) In both high and low tow positions the glider should not be allowed to get more than one tug wing span above or below it, as otherwise cable drag becomes excessive. (ii) The charts — Figs. 1 & 2 — show the relationship between the salient features of tug aircraft, as seen from the glider when flying in the BEST and LIMIT positions on both high and low tow. The true BEST and LIMIT positions will vary with tug loading and IAS, in particular in some conditions the LOW-BEST position as illustrated may be found to be on the edge of, or just within, the slipstream. The silhouettes, which are based on incidence angles at certain specific loadings and speeds, must therefore be taken as a general guide only. Pilots will find the most comfortable high and low tow positions by experience and, as it is tiring to maintain one position for long periods, some variation is permissible provided, generally, that the outline of the tug remains between the position depicted by the silhouettes marked BEST and LIMIT.

(11) *Level Flight:* (i) Small amounts of slack in the tow rope can be ignored but the control column should be

eased forward slightly to prevent snatch as the slack is taken up by the tug. If the slack is appreciable it should be taken up by easing the control column slightly back until the rope is almost taut, when the column should be eased forward to minimise snatch. (ii) On turns, keep directly behind (or slightly inside) the tug. (iii) *Cloud flying:* If cloud is entered the glider pilot should release tow immediately unless a tow cable angle indicator is fitted and authority has been given for blind flying.

(16) *Approach and Landing:* (i) Up to half flap may be used on the cross wind approach to regulate height. (ii) Make the final turn towards the landing ground with half

19

flap and when sure of getting into the landing ground, lower the flaps fully. (iii) The glide path with flaps fully down is steep, and care is necessary, especially in strong winds, not to get too far downwind. Flaps may be raised to the half down position if undershooting but it must be remembered that response is slow. Flaps must not be raised fully at normal flaps down approach speeds, and even if speed is increased in order to raise them fully, this will not correct undershooting at this stage of the approach. (iv) Recommended speeds for final straight approach, with flaps fully down are: Light (60 mph IAS), Heavy (75 to 80 mph IAS). (v) Flatten out and land on the main wheels in a slightly tail down attitude, lower the aircraft gently on to the nose wheel and then, when all three wheels are on the ground, apply brakes. *Note:* the brake action is not differential . . .

(17) *After Landing:* (i) Raise flaps. (ii) When being towed down-wind, controls should be held central, or if the glider is not occupied all control surfaces and the flaps must be locked. (iii) Park facing into wind with controls and flaps locked.

(18) *Emergencies:* (i) Although the tug pilot is CAPTAIN of the combination the glider pilot may, in emergency, cast off and take other action on his own initiative; he should; however, warn the tug pilot first if possible.

Above: *Waiting for the signal to take off.*
Right: *A British paratrooper with some of his kit.*

The First Day

17 September 1944

In a British glider

Glider Pilot Sergeant W. D. Green recalls:

'The Controller waved his green flag and our tug, a brand-new Dakota, started to taxi down the runway. Blown back in the slipstream of its propellers, pebbles spattered our windscreen as the slack tow rope in front of us twitched, then tautened. Seconds later our wheels were creaking, then rumbling as the glider gathered speed. As we were in the first wave which set off on Sunday, the 17th, we counted ourselves lucky. I was the second pilot.

'Our Horsa was carrying a 6-pdr gun and a jeep. The driver and the gunlayer crouched on the seats at the back of the glider. The Dakota climbed slowly. At 2000ft the ground fog thinned out to reveal a whole armada of gliders and towing planes stretching back into the far distance, where the tugs and gliders looked little bigger than mosquitoes. Flying a glider in the turbulence created by so many aircraft was hard physical work, but the pilot of our tug skilfully dodged other tug-glider combinations heading towards Holland by setting a course on the edge of the formation and at a different altitude. We knew he was taking a risk, but we were grateful and kept our finger crossed for him.

'We felt perfectly safe in the pilots' cabin. The only sensation of movement came from the wisps of cloud slipping past the glider. Our maps were of little help in trying to settle where we were over the sea or when we crossed the Dutch coast, as the Germans had flooded the islands in the Rhine delta and rubbed out some of the most recognisable features of the landscape. But eventually dry land appeared below us and I decided it was time to fix our position.

' "Hullo tug! How long before we reach our landing zone? Over".

' "Hullo, glider, this is tug. About another 15 minutes. Then you're on your own. Do you know where you are now? Over."

' "Thank you, tug. I would say we are just about over the mouth of the Rhine delta. Please confirm."

' "Correct. There are two more river crossings and then you ought to be able to spot the landing zone."

'From then on until we landed I had to keep a constant check on our location. From time to time AA guns below fired, but they didn't worry us very much. Then we passed over the mouth of the Maas and a blue network of canals spread out beneath us. It was much cooler now and I asked the first pilot for some of the hot tea from his thermos flask. There was a wry satisfaction in sitting back and supping tea while he had to sweat over the controls.

'In another 20 minutes we were over our turning point at 's Hertogenbosch and could see patches of ground fog below us. AA guns opened up. Flak was bursting around our tug, so the pilot turned to starboard and we found ourselves flying through thick cumulus.

'It was not long now before the Lower Rhine came into view and minutes later I spotted our landing zone at the junction of two tiny woods. I was amazed how easily recognisable it was; it looked just like the air photographs from which we had been briefed.

'Now came the moment to cast off the tow rope.

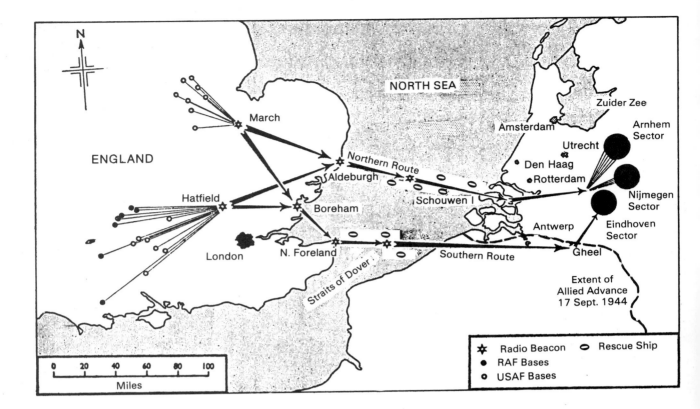

'I jerked the release lever, the rope zipped past us and the din of the wind outside dropped from a high-pitched whistle to a low hiss. In the sky around us we could see other gliders all heading towards the landing zone. We were still too high, so I pushed the flaps to the half-open position and the Horsa tipped forward like a sledge on a steep slope. Meantime our Dakota had turned away to starboard. As our speed decreased the noises outside diminished and in the pilots' cabin it all seemed very peaceful. Losing height slowly we crossed the river and could see in the distance the silhouette of the Arnhem bridge, the objective of the operation.

'Turning to starboard now, I opened the flaps to the full extent, the angle of descent increased and we sank downwards like a lift to float over a hedge and make a rough landing. The Horsa bounced once or twice as we braked hard, then we came to a standstill. For a few moments — until a rattle of distance machine gun fire brought us to our senses — we remained in our seats.

'Now we squeezed from the pilots' cabin aft into the main body. The rear section of the glider had to be separated before we could unload the jeep and trailer. To do this eight wing nuts had to be slackened simultaneously so the other pilot and I set about that, while three of the paratroops unfastened the chains securing the vehicles inside the glider. All of us were sweating like bulls, but as the shooting seemed to be getting closer there was clearly no time for a breather. Eventually the chains dropped off and all wing nuts had been unscrewed, so I yelled to the boys outside to fetch the two metal channels which acted as an unloading ramp.

'Two more screws and we had finished. But the tail was still firmly attached; we banged and bashed it from the inside, but it wouldn't budge. When I jumped out I found that the stupid clot who had fixed the rails had pushed them right under the rear end of the tail section. I threw my weight against it. Eventually the whole of the back end of the glider collapsed on to the rail, making it impossible to get the vehicles out. However, we all got under the tail section and after a struggle managed to heave it to one side. The rails were stuck in the ground, but they were still serviceable as some sort of ramp. We had made it! The driver took the wheel and drove the jeep and trailer out of the wrecked Horsa.

'The whole performance had taken just on 20 minutes — not bad considering what we saw happening elsewhere. All around us men were sweating and swearing as they heaved and hauled at the tails of their gliders; some were even using saws and axes.

'It was a chaotic scene, with people poring over maps and asking each other if they had seen any sign of this or that unit. To get to our own assembly area we had to jog along a narrow sandy path through low undergrowth, across fields and along the edge of a wood. In the fields all the way along the route we could see gliders. Some were even hanging in the trees, with their wings wedged in the branches; I saw at least one undercarriage upside down. There were bits of gliders everywhere.

'From time to time bullets crackled around our heads

Above: *A Horsa Mk II taking off: 'We were lucky to be among the first to go . . .'*

and everybody ducked when a mortar bomb whistled over. Eventually we were marshalled into some sort of order. Under the command of a para brigade officer and with each of us carrying packs weighing about a hundred pounds apiece we set off towards Arnhem. There was a good deal of grumbling about having to leave our jeeps behind as the long column marched down a shady tree-lined avenue. The further we went, the fiercer grew the bombardment and so our pace got correspondingly slower. We were at the rear of the column and were grateful for the breaks — sometimes as long as two hours — when the column halted. In any case we couldn't have kept up with the paratroops; they had much less to carry and could make a much quicker pace. To the sound of a battle raging somewhere around Arnhem, this was how we spent half the night.

'Then we were ordered to turn round and retrace our steps halfway back to our starting point, where we dug in along the railway line. Our orders were to defend the stretch of road down which we had marched and be prepared for an attack at dawn'.

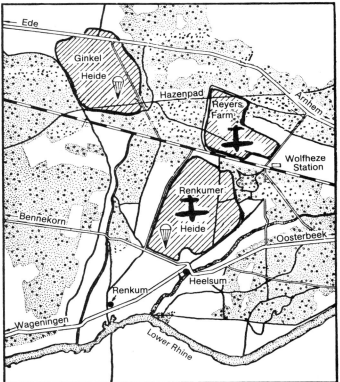

Above: *West of Arnhem on the afternoon of 17 September: The three landing zones.*

In a Dakota over Holland

American radio reporter Edward R. Murrow of CBS sent this despatch from a Dakota somewhere over Holland on that sunny Sunday afternoon of 17 September 1944:

'By now we are getting towards the dropping area and I sit looking down the length of the fuselage.

'The crew chief is on his knees back in the very rear talking into his inter-com, talking with the pilots. The rest of the men have folded up their yellow Mae Wests, as there is certainly no possibility of our ditching in the water on this trip. They're looking out of the window rather curiously, almost as though they were passengers on a peacetime airliner. You occasionally see a man rub the palm of his hand against his trouser leg. There seems to be just that-oh-sort of a film over some of their faces, as though they were just on the verge of perspiring, but they aren't. Every man the whole length of the ship is now looking down at this Dutch countryside. We see a few stacks down there that seem to be wheat. There's a small factory off to the right, about half of it demolished. The country is perfectly flat, of course; a little while ago we saw some of those big thirty-passenger British Horsa gliders being towed in, and it looks much better glider country than it did in Normandy.

'Suddenly the pilot called our attention to the parapacks coming out from the aircraft in front of us.

'There go the parapacks from the formation ahead of us — yellow, brown, red, drifting down gently, dropping their containers. I can't see, we're a little too far away — I can't see the bodies of the men — yes, I can, just like little brown dolls hanging under a green lamp-shade they look . . .

'Just before our men dropped we saw the first flak.

'I think it's coming from that little village just beside the canal. More tracer coming up now, just cutting across in front of our nose.

'They're just queued up on the door now, waiting to jump. Walking out of this aircraft with no flak suits, no armour plating on the ship, we're down just about to the drop altitude now — there are more tracers coming up — nine ships ahead of us have just dropped — you can see the men swinging down — in just about thirty seconds now our ship will drop and those fighting men will walk out on to Dutch soil — you can probably hear the snap as they check the lashing on the static line — there it goes. Do you hear them shout 3-4-5-6-7-8-9-10-11-12-13-14-15-16-17-18. There they go — every man out — I can see their 'chutes going down now — every man clear — they're dropping just beside a little windmill near a church — handing there very gracefully. They're all going down so slowly it seems as though they should get to the ground much faster. We're now swinging about making a right-hand turn.

'As we came out there was the blue grey haze of battle smoke. The parachutes dappled the green fields. And more planes and more gliders were going in. Only a few minutes after the drop we looked down and saw parachutists moving along the road towards a village.

Above left: *View of the Dutch coast from a pilot's cabin.*
Above right: *Dakotas with US Waco gliders.*
Below right: *American paratroops before take-off.*

They had formed up, were properly spaced, and were moving on their first objective.'

A 'Red Devil's' view

British paratrooper M. G. Sprider remembers how the operation looked to him:

' "Stand up! Hook on" shouted the despatcher. Quietly we checked our equipment. One after the other the men in front of me reported "OK". Then it was my turn. I was No 13 — which didn't exactly please me. Worse still, with all my equipment I looked like Father Christmas. I could hardly move a step. Ammunition bandoliers almost choked the life out of me, my pockets were full to bursting with handgrenades and rations, added to which I had a Sten machine carbine, a groundsheet, a blanket and a pack — and I also had to carry a reserve parachute and a folding bicycle.

'The Jerries were not doing much shooting but what

there was seemed pretty accurate. The C-47 flying right alongside us was hit amidships and I saw it crash in flames; nobody jumped from it. It seemed an age before our red lamp went on. That was the signal "Get ready to jump". The AA fire was getting steadily worse. At last the green light flashed on: we were over the dropping zone. As the chaps in front of me started to jump, I hobbled towards the door. It was almost my turn and the man in front of me was just about to jump, when he collapsed, fatally hit. The despatcher simply shoved his body aside and out I dived. I had almost got used to the roar of the engines inside the plane: the sudden silence now was uncanny. I felt a sudden tug as the static line yanked out the canopy and then I saw it billowing out snow-white above me.

'On flew our C-47, ejecting more paratroops. All their parachutes worked perfectly. It was 14.01hrs now and all around me was a fantastic shower of equipment panniers floating down to earth beneath brown, red and yellow parachutes.

'About a kilometre to my right I could see the roofs of the little town of Heelsum and behind it, in the distance, I caught a glimpse of silver — the Lower Rhine. Some ten kilometres in front of me was the dark silhouette of Arnhem. Then a sudden whistling and a few sharp cracks reminded me that this was no training exercise. Instinctively I pressed the folding bike against me and tried to make out where the shots were coming from — probably from the little wood on my left. The whistling did not stop and I saw a paratroop only about 25 metres away from me suddenly convulse, then drop his head — apparently lifeless. A dark stain spread over his back and then I could see blood running out of his boots.

'As the ground rushed up towards me I released my kit bag and let go of the folding bike. A moment later I landed on sandy soil and rolled over as I'd been taught. I wasted no time in getting rid of the parachute harness. The, releasing the safety catch on my Sten, I grabbed the bike and set off towards the assembly point. In the distance I could hear the rattle of machine guns and an occasional burst of machine pistol fire. The whole dropping zone was seething with green-clad figures all making for their respective assembly areas. Within minutes I was joined by more and more men, and in next to no time we were shaping into a queue. I looked at my watch: it was exactly 14.15hrs.'

The official Allied Summary
Late on the afternoon of Sunday, 17 September, the BBC in London reported the optimistic view of an unnamed senior Air Force officer, commanding an airborne formation, that the greatest airborne operation had taken place and would prove even more important and decisive than the D-Day landings. Its results, he said, would be far-reaching: success or failure would mean the difference between a quick decision and victory in the West or a long winter war. The Army, he concluded, was convinced that the airborne forces had been put down in the right place at the right moment.

The Allied Headquarters communique of Monday 18 September took the same view:

'Airborne army lands in Holland — Several Towns Reported occupied — Operation "Like Clockwork" — Simultaneous advance by Second Army.

'Strong forces of the First Allied Airborne Army landed in Holland yesterday afternoon, and last night pilots reported that the operation "went like clockwork." One report states that the enemy has been cleared from several Dutch towns.

'It was the greatest airborne operation ever launched, more than 1,000 aircraft taking part. R.A.F. and American bombers prepared the way with massive night and day bombing attacks on airfields, gun positions and barracks.

Top left: *The approach.*
Top right: *The despatcher called: 'Stand up hook on!'*
Far left: *'Out I dived . . .'*
Left: *'. . . then I saw the canopy billowing snow white above me.'*
Above: *'On flew our C-47, ejecting more paratroops.'*

27

'Last night it was reported that armoured spearheads of the British Second Army had moved forward from their Beeringen bridgehead and had advanced two miles across the Dutch frontier.' (*The Times*, London, 18.9.1944)

The German reaction

SS-Obersturmführer Walter Harzer of the 9th SS-Panzer Division recorded the start of the battle in this report:

'Sunday, September 17, has been a splendid day. Because we had a ceremony to present Knights Crosses to men of the 9th SS-Panzer Division the divisional commander was able to watch the first (enemy) airborne landings. Initially we assumed that a powerful daylight bombing force was on its way to attack targets in Germany — quite a common sight these days — so the usual AA fire created little concern. However at 13.30hrs the first enemy parachutists were dropped and II SS-PzAK (the Corps Reconnaissance Unit) promptly alerted my divisional headquarters. (I received this warning order while I was at the tactical headquarters of my divisional AA regiment). Divisional Headquarters in turn relayed the message and told all units to prepare for action. Meantime I was on my way back to the divisional command post at Beekbergen. Within an hour most units except for SS-PzAA9 (the 9th AA Bn) had reported they were ready to move. It took the 9th AA Bn another hour to get ready because they had to replace the tracks on the armoured vehicles I had reported unserviceable and so unfit for transfer to the 10th SS-Panzer Division.

'The Intelligence Officer told me that the main enemy thrusts appeared to be directed towards Arnhem, from the west, and Nijmegen, where parachutists and glider-borne troops had landed in strength. German forces in the vicinity of both places had already been deployed. About 16.00hrs a message from II SS-Panzer Korps HQ ordered "Group Harzer to concentrate in the Velp area and prepare to counter-attack an enemy force which has landed at Oosterbeek, west of Arnhem." '

The official German summary

The German view of the first day's events was summarised in a German High Command communique of 18 September 1944:

'Following intensive air attacks enemy airborne troops yesterday landed on Dutch soil behind our front lines in the Arnhem, Eindhoven and Nijmegen areas. During the afternoon other enemy forces launched attacks in the Antwerp-Maastricht region in order to establish contact with the airborne invaders. Bitter fighting developed, especially around Neerpelt, but the enemy was able to make little progress in a northerly direction. Massive counter-attacks have been mounted against the airborne forces, and between Maastricht and Aachen our troops are continuing to resist the powerful assault which is being thrown against them. In other sections of the Western Front several minor attacks by the enemy have been smashed.'

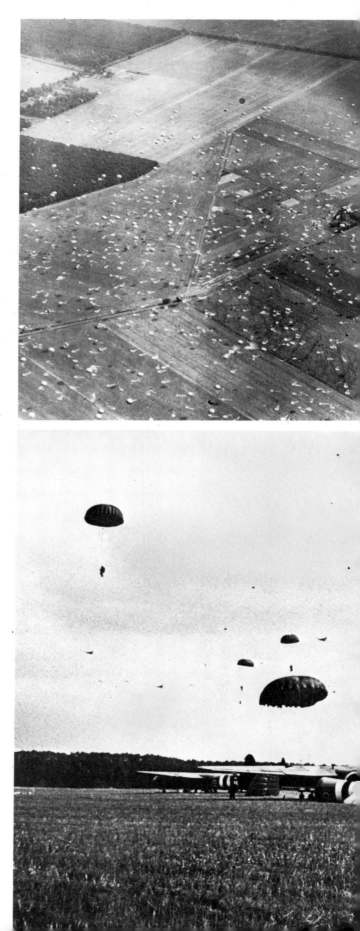

Left and top left: *17 September 1944, paratroops and gliders between Wolfheze and Heelsum.*
Top centre: *Landed! A paratroop and container.*
Top right: *Horsa Mk II after landing.*
Above: *An unloaded Horsa Mk II.*

29

The course of the battle

On the morning of 17 September, 1944, 1400 bombers had taken off from 26 airfields in the south of England to soften up the dropping zones in Holland and destroy the German AA positions. About noon they were followed by another 2023 planes — transports filled with paratroops and other aircraft towing Horsa, Waco* and giant Hamilcar gliders, flying at an altitude of only 500metres (the Hamilcar, with a payload of 8 tons, was capable of carrying infantry, artillery, vehicles, ammunition and supplies). With 20,000 men aboard, this was the most imposing air armada in history. More aircraft and more gliders took the air later and during the next two days they were to be in continuous circuit. Some 1500 fighters — Mustangs, Lightnings, Spitfires, Typhons, Tempests and Mosquitos — swarmed around the huge fleet. Altogether 5000 planes filled the skies above Holland. In his headquarters at Vught, near 's Hertogenbosch, General Student, who four years before had himself dropped on Holland with a much smaller airborne force, gazed up at the armada, lost in admiration at the scale of the operation.

Not a single German fighter came up to attack and the reaction of the German AA defences, which had suffered heavily in the attacks preceding the airborne assault, was surprisingly mild. The defences destroyed 35 transports, 13 gliders and about 30 other aircraft, but the total was far less than it should have been.

As the first of the Market Garden planes was crossing the Dutch coast, Model, Commander of Army Group B, received an urgent message from Fieldmarshal von Runstedt. Did the signs indicate to Model that an airborne and seaborne invasion of northern Holland was imminent? The general situation and a recent increase in enemy air reconnaissance activity suggested that it was a decided possibility. Model was told to transmit his conclusions immediately to OKW (ie, to Hitler's headquarters).

On that morning of 17 September Model was attending a conference in the Park Hotel Hartenstein, after which he and his staff adjourned to the Hotel Tafelberg for lunch. About 14.00hrs there was an air raid. With bombs dropping around the hotel and its windows shattering, the Fieldmarshal dived to the ground. 'We're in a pickle', his operations officer Colonel von Tempelhoff told him, 'there's a division or two of enemy paratroops overhead!' At that Model ordered everybody to evacuate the hotel and rendezvous at Terborg. The Fieldmarshal hurried away to the headquarters of SS-Obergruppenführer Bittrich's II Panzer Corps, under the impression that the airborne troops were merely commandos on a kidnapping expedition, their objective his HQ and his own person. Bittrich, on the other hand, had a hunch something much bigger was afoot. So it was the Obergruppenführer, not the Fieldmarshal, who ordered everybody to stand-to

* *Translator's Note: The British name for the Waco CG-4A was Hadrian.*

Left: *A miniature motorcycle, weighing only 27lb.*
Above: *'Landings completed, negligible resistance.'*
Below left: *Lt-Colonel John Frost* (right).
Below centre: *A formation of Stirlings drops supply panniers in the Arnhem area.*

and despatched his Panzer-Grenadiers to secure the Arnhem road-bridge.

The British landed only a stone's throw from Model's headquarters. Had they appreciated this and captured Model, as he thought they were intent on doing, they would have eliminated the German best equipped to organise their destruction. Instead Model, as C-in-C, was able to start drafting the plans that would systematically defeat and destroy Market Garden.

The summary Allied report at the end of the first day had a note of triumph: 'Landings accomplished. Virtually no resistance.' Taylor's US 101st Airborne Division had dropped between Veghel and Zon, Gavin's US 82nd Airborne south of Nijmegen, and Urquhart's British 1st Airborne Division on the far side of the Rhine (ie, north of the river) to the west of Arnhem. But after a text-book drop, the units were slow to assemble. The British paratroops were far too methodical; they did not seem to appreciate that in modern war audacity usually achieves more than discretion.

Nor did the civilian population help the operation to run smoothly. Wild with joy, the Dutch streamed out of their houses to offer the invaders a cup of tea, and the British soldiers succumbed to pleas to autograph books and papers, to take photos and to socialise with the girls. When the 'Red Devils' at last managed to extricate themselves from this frenetic welcome they faced a long march of ten kilometres to their objective, because the 1st Airborne Division's dropping zone had been located so far from Arnhem. Consequently the division could not devote all its energy and resources to capture and hold the vital bridge across the Lower Rhine in the first 24 hours of the operation; instead, precious time was lost and men frittered away in street fighting inside the town.

By noon on 17 September Horrocks' XXX Corps on the British 2nd Army had broken out of its bridgehead around Neerpelt on the north bank of the Albert Canal in Belgium and its armour was driving down the tarmac road towards Eindhoven. But the Germans had blocked this road in a number of places with anti-tank artillery and tank traps. There were about 20,000 vehicles in General Horrocks' force, with tanks of the Irish Guards as the spearhead. This vanguard soon ran into trouble at a spot where, according to air reconnaissance reports, there should have been no enemy. The leading tanks were surprised and blasted out of action, 'their steel hulks effectively blocking the road to any further advance by Horrocks' column.

This put General Taylor, commanding the US 101st Division on the spot. To make his force as mobile as possible Taylor had elected to fly in with jeeps rather than artillery. With the British now stymied on the Eindhoven road, the armoured support on which Taylor was relying to hold his 15mile stretch of corridor would be stalled, leaving him awkwardly placed. At this time he had no idea that General Student's command post was less than 10 miles from the 101st dropping zone, nor that reinforcements for von Zangen's 15th Army had dug in near Tilburg.

About now Urquhart drove in his jeep to Brig Philip Hick's 1st Airlanding Brigade tactical headquarters. Awaiting him was news destined to have a decisive effect on the whole operation. Major Freddie Gough's Armoured Reconnaissance Squadron, which was to make the initial assault on the Arnhem Bridge, had been unable to start the attack because the gliders carrying the squadron's armoured jeeps had not landed on the proper landing zone. Nobody knew where they were. Nevertheless, Brig Lathbury's 1st Parachute Brigade now set off towards the objective, according to plan, while Brig Hackett's 4th Parachute Brigade took up defensive positions around the landing zone. Near Oosterbeek two battalions of the 1st Parachute Bde were halted by an SS unit and heavy fighting developed, so that execution of the divisional plan now devolved on the remaining battalion commanded by Lt-Col C. D. Frost.

As his battalion marched towards Heveadorp, a small place on the north bank of the Lower Rhine, Frost was unaware of the existence, a few hundred metres to his right, of a cable ferry that linked Heveadorp with the village of Driel on the south bank of the river. Frost's commander, General Urquhart did not know of it either, yet it could have been instrumental in capturing the

Arnhem bridge; with it the paratroops could have crossed the river within a few hours of their landing and taken the bridge by assaulting it from the south. Despite poring over thousands of aerial photographs the planners seem to have missed the Driel ferry completely.

The railway bridge was blown up just before a detachment from Frost's battalion got to it. Meanwhile Frost had detached 'B' Company and sent them to subdue German machine-gunners on the high ground called Den Brink. 'B' Company also had orders to capture the pontoon bridge across the Rhine between the road and railway bridges, but the Germans had by now dismantled part of the pontoon bridge and towed away some of the barges to a river dock east of Arnhem.

With the 1st Parachute Brigade already experiencing a foretaste of things to come Urquhart returned to this tactical headquarters. There he learned that the airborne signallers were having little or no luck with their radios. Contact with the 1st Parachute Brigade had been lost and there was no communication with London. Nothing had been heard, either, from the 2nd Battalion, which

Above right: *Over Arnhem.*
Below: *As often happened the Dutch came out to watch the unloading of a US Waco glider.*
Below right: *The 'Red Devils'.*

33

was closing in on the bridge. Realising that it might take hours to get a reply to the messages already transmitted, Urquhart resolved to find out for himself what was going on. With a signaller he set out in a jeep intending to locate Lathbury, the 1st Parachute Brigade commander. While they were driving along the signaller tried repeatedly to contact Frost's battalion, but the radio stayed dead until they were some way down the Arnhem-Utrecht road. Then the signaller did pick up a signal which he thought came from the 2nd Battalion. But he was wrong; it was a German station.

With the fighting only just begun the British communication system was already a serious casualty. The closer the paratroops got to Arnhem, in fact, the more their radio communications deteriorated. The 22 set was supposed to have a range of more than 5 miles; but transmissions from Lathbury's battalions and Gough's recce unit, barely 3 miles from Divisional HQ, were weak and erratic. An American detachment with a more powerful HF set had been sent in with Urquhart to maintain ground-to-air communication with the fighter bombers on call for the close support of the airborne troops, but this set proved as useless as the others, unhappily it had been tuned to a different frequency from that of the fighter bombers. If ground-to-air communication had been efficient in the early hours of the operation, there is little doubt that Allied air support could have exerted a decisive influence on the land battle. The signallers at Corps HQ did succeed in establishing radio contact with the 2nd Army and with base in the United Kingdom, but not with the 1st Airborne Division. The outcome of Operation Market Garden was already in doubt.

For its part, the 1st Airborne Division had no means of getting in touch with Browning's Corps HQ near Nijmegen, nor with Montgomery's Intelligence staff. And communication with England was possible only through the set of a BBC radio reporter operating with the division; even this was subject to interference from a powerful German station operating on the same wavelength. So while Urquhart could pick up UK transmissions, his own signals were not getting through. Messages had to pass to London by way of the BBC man's set and then be relayed back to Browning's headquarters; by the time Browning's staff had drafted a reply and this had been sent back to London for retransmission to the 1st Airborne Division, hours had elapsed and the battle situation had changed completely.

On the German side the recovery and repair unit of the 9th SS-Panzer Division had been working like beavers. The dismantled tank tracks had been replaced and all the supposedly unserviceable armoured vehicles that were to have been handed over to the 10th SS-Pz Division Hohenstaufen had been put back on the road within a record two hours. That done, Harzer ordered Haupsturmführer Gräbner, the commander of the division's armoured reconnaissance unit, to reconnoitre and determine enemy strength in the area bounded by Hoenderloo barracks north of Arnhem and Nijmegen in

Above and above right: *The Allied liberators get a delighted reception from the inhabitants. No one had allowed for the enthusiasm of the Dutch, which upset the time-table and hampered the smooth evolution of the operation.*
Below right: *On the way to Arnhem: Glider pilot Captain Ogilvie* (right).

the south. After driving from one end of Arnhem to the other, Gräbner's vehicles found the town deserted. Shortly before 1900 hrs they crossed the great road bridge and carried on towards Nijmegen. 'No sign of the enemy', Gräbner reported over his radio, so he was told to return.

Harzer was usually so meticulous that it is incredible he did not instruct Gräbner to secure the Arnhem road bridge, particularly as Bittrich had issued an explicit order laying down that 'the aim is to occupy and firmly hold the bridge at Arnhem'. Even as Gräbner was probing towards Nijmegen and away from Arnhem, Frost's men were advancing through the outskirts of Arnhem towards the bridge. Gräbner's recce party and the vanguard of Frost's battalion missed each other by about an hour, during which the bridge itself was left unguarded and empty. However, less than 25 minutes before Frost's 'A' Company reached the northern approach of the bridge SS-Panzergrenadiers were in position on both banks of the river and the bridge was firmly in their hands.

Frost took a few men from his headquarters company to march with 'A' Company towards the bridge. At 19.45 hrs they emerged from Rodenburg Street on to the Riynkade. Moving cautiously, the Red Devils continued in an easterly direction — and there, suddenly, was the Arnhem road bridge, intact and undamaged! The 25

Far left: *First prisoners — surprise on both sides.*
Above right: *Oosterbeek: the British airborne troops still have more than 6 miles to march.*
Left: *Russians among the German prisoners.*

elderly 'Fieldgreys'* guarding the bridge were more interested in sleeping than fighting; earlier that afternoon they had left their posts.

Frost ought now to have stormed both ends of the bridge, but instead he sent out only one of 'A' Company's platoons. Immediately a quick-firing German AA gun opened up from a position on the north side and then the platoon ran into a hail of bullets from the machine guns of an armoured car at the other end. Frost and the rest of his men were stuck at the north end of the bridge; they would never be able to cross the river now.

SS-Sturmbannführer Krafft, the commander of a reserve battalion of Panzergrenadiers, had earlier found

* *Translator's Note: Feldgrauen* — a term used to distinguish the Wehrmacht (whose infantry wore grey) from the other services: in this case the Waffen SS.

himself and his unit on the very edge of a British landing zone. He was billeted in the Wolfheze hotel, less than a kilometre from Renkumer Heath, and two of his Panzergrenadier companies were in bivouacs on the heath near the road. The three parachute battalions had set out for Arnhem down three converging roads. The Wolfheze-Arnhem railway line ran almost at right angles between the northernmost of the three roads and that in the middle, and Sturmbannführer Krafft positioned his Panzergrenadiers along its tack so as to block the enemy advance on both flanks. However, Dobie's 1st Parachute Battalion slipped unnoticed past the German left (ie, northern) flank; neither side had seen anything — or hardly anything of each other, so Krafft was unaware of Dobie's move, and also that on the southernmost road Frost's 2nd Parachute Battalion had reached Arnhem and got as far as the Bridge with little opposition. In his turn, Frost had no idea that the Germans had closed in behind him and that he would eventually be cut off from the rest of the British Airborne Division.

Around 18.00hrs the Divisional Commander, General Urquhart, at last caught up with Lathbury, who had attached himself to Fitch's 3rd Battalion, and the two of them decided to stay with the battalion overnight. Both Urquhart and Lathbury were still deluded by the optimistic forecasts of negligible German resistance; both of them wanted to be on the spot when their troops reached the objective, the Arnhem road bridge. So it was that at the critical period the two most senior British commanders found themselves in the middle of a battle without staff and out of contact with the remainder of the force. Two of their three battalions (those of Dobie and Fitch) had been stopped and pinned down by enemy Panzer troops. Frost's 2nd Battalion was the only one to have reached the bridge. Lathbury heard this at about 17.30hrs and sent a message to his brigade staff telling them to take the road followed by the 2nd Battalion; ultimately they joined up with Frost near the bridge and came under his command.

Meantime Frost had assumed his 'B' Company had dealt with the Germans on the high ground at Den Brink and gone on to capture the pontoon bridge. He proposed to tell 'B' Company commander next to cross the Rhine in some of the boats which he could see in the little river dock near the pontoon bridge, so as to be in a position to attack the southern end of the bridge from the opposite bank. But with no radio contact between 'C' and 'B' Company Frost had to send runners out with his orders. They could not find 'B' Company anywhere near the pontoon bridge. Not until 05.00hrs next morning could they fight their way back to Battalion headquarters to report.

The Allies were not to know of the Germans' biggest prize: a complete copy of the Allied operation orders for Market Garden found in the wreck of an American Waco glider shot down near Vught. 'A translated and evaluated version of this extremely valuable document was on my desk a few hours later', General Student wrote later.

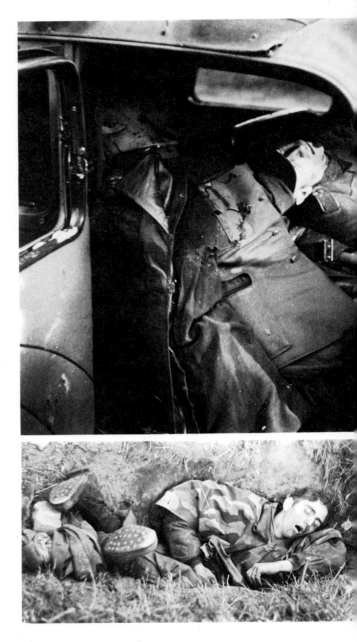

Wolfheze, the first casualties: the town commander of Arnhem Major-General Kussin (top), *his driver* (above right) *and a German soldier* (above).
Below right: *Tough soldiers of 10th SS-Panzer Division.*

Top: *Oosterbeek, the long march to Arnhem: a 6-pr anti-tank gun.*
Above: *Portable radio — not working.*
Below right: *Killed in action.*

The Second Day

18 September 1944

The official Allied Summary

On Tuesday 19 September 1944 Allied Headquarters issued a communiqué covering the events of the previous day:

'British armour reaches airborne troops — Reinforcements poured into Holland — Second Army beyond Eindhoven — A Boulogne fortress falls to Canadians.

'Airborne troops and supplies were still being poured into Holland yesterday, and the First Airborne Army has gained its initial objectives and taken prisoners.

'The first advanced armoured patrols of the British Second Army driving north from the Belgian border have established contact with the airborne forces. The Second Army, by-passing Eindhoven, has advanced 15 miles in just over 24 hours.

'In the fight for Boulogne the fortress of Mont Lambert surrendered yesterday to the Canadians, who now hold most of the town east of the river. On the American Third Army front General Patton's tanks are 18 miles beyond Nancy.' (*The Times*, London, 19.9.1944)

In the issue of 19 September the London *Times* also said:

'One of the officers expressed the belief, based on the operations now proceeding, that, given sufficient fighter cover and support to overcome *Flak*, the Siegfried line and the Rhine could be "jumped." The Airborne Army, he added, could tackle any task it was called upon to undertake...

'For the airborne operation 24 tons of maps were used; every soldier who landed had a map of the area in which he was to operate. In contrast with former airborne operations, parachute and glider-borne troops had all to be dropped in pin-pointed areas, not in districts as in Normandy, Italy, and elsewhere. This ensured concentrations of troops at stipulated objectives...

'Each dropping zone was marked by pathfinders only 15 minutes before the task forces arrived; every parachutist, with the exception of about a dozen, was dropped in his correct zone.'

The official German summary

On 19 September the German High Command described the events of the previous day thus:

"Reinforcements were dropped and landed in central Holland to support the enemy airborne forces operating behind our lines. Our own counter-attacks against the landing zones are slowly gaining ground despite determined enemy resistance. A powerful armoured thrust northwards by the enemy from his bridgehead at Neerpelt has reached Eindhoven; 43 enemy tanks have been destroyed in bitter fighting at close quarters. Northwest of Aachen the enemy has made little progress, in spite of large numbers of tanks and artillery which he has thrown into the battle. West and south of the town a number of enemy attacks have been repulsed and our counter-attacks in the Luneville area have been successful. On all other sectors of the front minor engagements only have been reported yesterday, but Boulogne and Brest were again bombarded by artillery and from the air."

The course of the battle

By the early morning of Monday 18 September four battalions of the Airborne Division were trying to get at the bridge, moving independently, but all operating in the same area between Arnhem's St Elizabeth Hospital and Rhine Pavilion. Fitch's 3rd Battalion was advancing up the road near the Rhine that Frost had taken to the bridge on Sunday, totally unaware of the presence of the other three battalions — Dobie's 1st Parachute Bn, Lea's 11th and McCardie's 2nd South Staffords — although only a few hundred yards in fact separated Fitch's battalion from Dobie's.

Urquhart and Lathbury, accompanying Fitch's battalion, became involved in street fighting near the St Elizabeth Hospital and had to take cover in a nearby house. A little while later Lathbury was hit by a burst from a German machine-gun and had to be left in the care of a brave Dutch couple. Urquhart and two young officers with him moved on, but the area was so full of Germans that they were soon forced to hide in Zwarteweg 14, a house owned by Anton Derksen. During the night a self-propelled gun parked outside the door of the house, so General Urquhart and his companions hurried upstairs to the attic, where there was only enough space for them to lie flat.

Between 09.00 and 10.00hrs that morning the Germans put up approximately 190 fighters to patrol the skies above Holland ready to intercept the second airborne lift. Dunkirk, still occupied by the Germans, lay below the air lane taken by the Allied transport planes, so early warning reports from here together with the information gleaned from the plans captured on 17 September enabled the Germans to lay on a warm reception hours in advance.

But in the event no Allied planes appeared. The weather in Holland was fine and sunny enough, but the base airfields in Britain were blanketed by thick fog. It was the middle of the afternoon before the second wave of transport aircraft crossed the North Sea and by then more than half of the German fighters were on the ground refuelling or flying back to their airfields for the same purpose. Such German fighters as were still in the vicinity could not penetrate the screen of fighter escorts protecting the Allied transports over Eindhoven and Arnhem. Around the dropping zone at Ginkel Heath, west of the railway station at Wolfheze, though, a fierce battle developed. SS troops with anti-aircraft guns had been sent from Arnhem to give the British a hot time as they came in and some 20 Messerschmitts and Focke-Wulfs also flew in at low level to disrupt the landings; in one sector alone 50 gliders went up in flames.

Underestimating the fighting potential of the German troops in the region had been a terrible blunder, for the presence near Arnhem of the two Waffen SS-Panzer divisions, undetected by Allied air reconnaissance, was proving disastrous to the 1st Airborne Division. Hitler had ordered everybody capable of carrying arms to be thrown into the fray; one battalion brought to battle was composed entirely of disabled soldiers and commanded

AIRBORNE ARMY LANDS IN HOLLAND

◆

SEVERAL TOWNS REPORTED OCCUPIED

OPERATION "LIKE CLOCKWORK"

SIMULTANEOUS ADVANCE BY SECOND ARMY

Strong forces of the First Allied Airborne Army landed in Holland yesterday afternoon, and last night pilots reported that the operation " went like clockwork." One report states that the enemy has been cleared from several Dutch towns.

It was the greatest airborne operation ever launched, more than 1,000 aircraft taking part. R.A.F. and American bombers prepared the way with massive night and day bombing attacks on airfields, gun positions, and barracks.

Last night it was reported that armoured spearheads of the British Second Army had moved forward from their Beeringen bridgehead and had advanced two miles across the Dutch frontier.

Top: *Excerpt from* The Times *of 18.9.1944.*
Above: *Brigadier Philip Hicks.*
Right: *A page of the* Daily Mail *of September 18, 1944.*

Daily Mail

NO. 15,094   ONE PENNY   FOR KING AND EMPIRE   MONDAY, SEPTEMBER 18, 1944

4 A.M. EDITION

GREAT SKY ARMY OPENS BATTLE FOR RHINE

THE R.A.F. and British Airborne and Parachute units played a big part in the operation. Here a R.A.F. Halifax is towing British Horsa gliders over the Rhine as the great air army flew deep into Holland, by-passing flooded areas and turning the German line.   A GUNNER in an escorting aircraft keeps watch for enemy fighters as part of the Allied armada in perfect formation crosses the coast of Holland, was slight, although some enemy fighters did try to break through.

Dutch Towns Taken in First Hours: Fierce Fighting

EARLY to-day there was every indication that the first stage of the great airborne invasion of Holland had gone entirely to plan. A number of Dutch towns have already been captured, and Lt.-General L. Brereton, commander of the attacking 1st Airborne Army, and his staff were described by one war correspondent last night as "highly elated" at the success of the operation.

One staff officer of Troop Carrier Command described the landing as "successful beyond all expectation." It is believed that very few of the troop-carriers were lost to enemy fighters or A.A. fire.

To-day the Airborne Army, together with the British 2nd Army, was engaged in what may well prove to be the final, decisive battle of Germany—Major-General Paul Williams, commander of the troop-carriers, yesterday described the attack as "the knock-out blow to the already staggering enemy."

The air army swooped across the water-belt of Holland, the strongest defensive position in Western Europe. Success in the battle now raging will mean that they have turned the line of the Rhine, the Reich's last defence.

ZERO HOUR—LUNCH TIME

Before R.A.F. crews took off they were told: " You are about to take part in an airborne operation transcending in importance even the one launched on D-Day. It is an operation vital to the outcome of the land battle. Success may mean all the difference between a rapid decision in the west and a protracted winter campaign.

" The Army is relying implicitly on us to drop the men in sufficient numbers at the right place at the right time."

Up to early to-day there was little detailed news of the airborne army, but it is known that it encountered heavy opposition in many places. Even at these points, however, the paratroops and gliders made good landings.

General Eisenhower's H.Q. is maintaining strict secrecy about the movements of the air army, but the Germans declare that the landings were made in the areas of Tilburg, Eindhoven, and Nijmegen, and on the northern bank of the Rhine, west of the German border.

The three places named are all important communication centres in an area which, according to Berlin, is only a few miles ahead of the spearhead of the Second Army, which yesterday launched a heavy tank assault towards Eindhoven.

Rail Strike in Holland

Daily Mail Radio Station

A general strike on the Dutch railways was ordered by the Netherlands Government in a broadcast last night from Radio Orange.

The broadcast said : "This order is of paramount importance Do well and long!"

This was followed by a call from Central Eisenhower to the officers and men of the German armed forces which said : "Dutch Troops of the Interior right side by side with the Allied armies.

" These troops enjoy the same rights and privileges as do Regular soldiers, and the same laws apply to them. They are under my supreme command.

" They have their own officers, and are under the command of Prince Bernhard."

Little Flak

Flares hung in the sky. Flak from the enemy guns was meagre.

Early this morning guns as far away as Cap Gris Nez were firing towards Boulogne The flashes from the gun, were almost incessant. Coastal batteries were firing seawards, and occasionally the bursts in the water could be seen from the coast.

The fighting seemed to have reached Wimereux—which gave particular pleasure to the watchers since it is from Wimereux that the cross-Channel guns have been firing towards the Dover area.

One peculiarity of the battle was that, although there were tremendous explosions across the water, little could be heard of them.

Nazi Attache's Trip

Lisbon, Sunday.—Col. von Kaulbach, German Military Attache in Lisbon has left for Spain by air.—Exchange.

BACK PAGE—Col THREE

Armada Flew in Fighter 'Tunnel'

LINE-UP LIKE CARS

FLYING out of the haze like bees swarming from a hive came hundreds upon hundreds of Allied planes. To the sides, above, and below them were fighters, forming an armoured tunnel in the air above Holland.

Through this tunnel the men of the First Allied Airborne Army flew to their destination yesterday, the low-flying transports in rigid formation within the swarm of fighters.

That was how one correspondent, William Downs, of CBS, saw the start of the great air invasion of the Netherlands—" One of the most tremendous sights I have ever seen in four years of covering this war."

It was ideal weather for the job. Low clouds gave cover for the unarmed C-47 troop-carrier planes.

Over the paratroop-drop zones and glider-landing sites the clouds lifted, giving the pilots perfect visibility.

Before the air armada arrived fighters and fighter-bombers had blasted the picked areas, going down in "suicide" dives on the German gun positions. Eighth Air Force fighters radioed a "running commentary" to their headquarters, telling of fierce battles in the air.

Though some units ran into fierce opposition, one observer after another told how thoroughly the planes that smashed a way in had done their work.

" The odd gun I saw fire never got in more than a single round before these fighters had shut it quiet," said a tow pilot. "I never saw anything so fast. I would not be a Hun ack-ack gunner for all the money in the world."

Down from a reconnaissance flight, low over the British and American fighters, a Spitfire pilot said : " The gliders were laid out on the landing zones as if they had been placed there by hand. There was all bang in the right spot, and unloading was going on.

" In one place I got right down and saw the local people, out on their Sunday best, lending a hand with the unloading. In another the troops were already jamming over an orchard wall talking to a crowd of airs."

With the hundreds of homebased fighters flew across the North Sea were Dutch pilots flying Spitfires, Tempests, and Mustangs of R.A.F., 2nd T.A.F., and A.D.G.B.

Their Day

The acting squadron commander of an all-Dutch squadron said it was the day his squadron had been awaiting for four years.

" And it came as a tremendous surprise," he added. " Imagine my reaction when I saw on the instructions 'Invasion of Holland.'"

Lee Disher, B.U.P correspondent, got this 'grand-stand' picture of the landings from a fighter pilot.

" The transports came by in perfect formation, strung out from their base to the target—some going and some coming. There was little opposition from German A.A positions which we had previously silenced.

" The paratroops dropped from their planes as if shot from guns, and at times I could see as many as nine in the air. Their manycoloured parachutes made a picturesque scene.

" Following up the paratroops I could see waves of big bombers towing gliders which landed in a field much like cars parked in a large one alongside the other and in neat straight rows

" Everything was quiet on the ground. There was nobody on the

BACK PAGE—Col FIVE

ARMOURED DRIVE INTO HOLLAND

From EDWARD GILLING

WITH THE SECOND ARMY, Sunday.

BRITISH armour has begun to roll again. While the airborne troops were being dropped into Holland to-day the Second Army launched attacks from its bridgehead over the Escaut Canal.

Rocket - firing Typhoons and hanter-bombers smashed down on the German defensive positions as our tanks went speeding along the roads into Holland

Cromwells and Shermans roared along the road with the carrierborne infantry following up

Hitherto only armoured car patrols had crossed the border, but to-day we were using our armoured strength.

This meant that the period of building up our supplies and stores that had been going on for nearly a fortnight had ended.

I watched one of our armoured columns move out from the bridgehead near the Groote along the Bolhoven road, and within one hour they were reported to be two miles inside Holland.

The attack was preceded by an artillery barrage against the enemy positions round the bridgehead.—Exchange.

Germans Raid Rome

Rome, Sunday German planes raided Rome for the first time in strength to-day, dropping bombs in the outskirts, U.S. fighters pursued them.—B.U.P.

RAF GO OUT AGAIN

Berlin has yet to tell Germany of the airborne attack on Holland.

Coast Crowd Sees Battle for Boulogne

From Folkestone

Canadian troops yesterday launched an all-out attack on Boulogne, after a four-hours R.A.F. blitz. But last night they had made good progress.—Story in BACK Page.

FOR hours after darkness fell last night people on Folkestone Leas watched the battle for Boulogne. The calm sea was illuminated almost to the Holland side of the Channel by terrific flashes on the French coast.

Coastal searchlights at Calais, Cap Gris Nez, and near Boulogne swept the Channel except the particularly big one cost a large light over the sea. Clouds of smoke could be seen rising from the haze

Bombers appeared to have joined in the battle for great bomb flashes could be seen.

London Alert in Dim-out

Londoners relaxed a little from the war last night and prepared to enjoy the dim-out. Then, not so long before an Alert sounded—believed to be due to a flying-bomb warning

When the Alert sounded police and wardens had a busy time warning people to black-out their houses again.

Lights On—and Off, with Picture.—Page THREE.

Brussels Cheers for 'Monty'

BRUSSELS, Sunday—Field-Marshal Montgomery attended a large church parade at Christ Church, in Brussels, this morning

Crowds lined the streets to give the British C-in-C a tremendous welcome as he drove away from the church.—Reuter.

FINNS REPORT ON REICH

(Daily Mail Exclusive)

FINNISH Army officers—in Berlin only a few days ago—have just presented a report on Germany's internal situation to their Government in Helsinki. Revealing extracts from it appear in Page TWO to-day.

43

by a one-legged major on crutches.

Twenty-four hours after the start of Operation Market Garden the Guards Armoured Division joined hands with General Taylor's American airborne troops. And so, one day behind schedule, the armour reached the southern outskirts of Eindhoven, only to be further delayed by the town's jubilant inhabitants. A full four hours elapsed before the Guards got through the town and were moving north again. Soon afterwards they were held up yet again near Son, where the Germans had blown a bridge. Fortunately it was soon realised that the bridge was not irreparably damaged and it was quickly patched up sufficiently for some purposes; but until heavy bridging material could be brought up, the Market Garden route north through Son was unusable by heavy vehicles.

On 18 September people in England had no idea of the real situation in and around Arnhem. Of the six airborne battalions that had been landed in the area, only Frost's 2nd Parachute Battalion had been able to get anywhere near the operational objective, the Arnhem bridge. More airborne reinforcements could not be sent because of the thick fog covering England. The men who had reached Arnhem were slowly congregating around Oosterbeek, where the hotel had served as Fieldmarshal Model's headquarters; here they concentrated in a perimeter and prepared for all-round defence.

During the afternoon of 18 September the Germans adopted new tactics. In an attempt to smoke Frost's paratroops out of the houses they were occupying at the north end of the bridge they hurled phosphorus grenades into the British positions. Frost's men were now virtually isolated, as all links with other units of the Airborne Division had been severed by a series of vigorous German assaults. Moreover German reinforcements were arriving on the scene almost hourly. The Battle of Arnhem had entered its definitive phase.

In sum, 24 hours after the launch of the operation, the British were encircled at Arnhem, with their commander, General Urquhart, the only man who might have been able to cope with the situation, helpless in an attic behind the German lines.

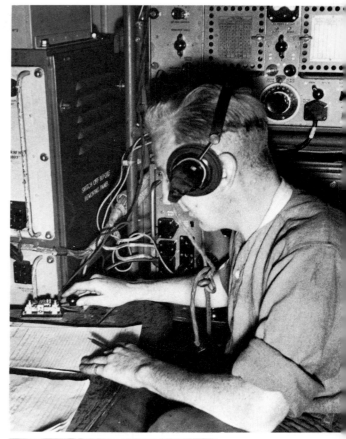

Top: *Unable to get through.*
Above: *Lieutenant-General Harmel.*
Above right: *The pontoon bridge cannot be located.*
Below right: *18 September 1944, 1. Zwarteweg 44 — General Urquhart's hiding place; in front of the corner building one can see the German self-propelled gun. 2. St Elizabeth Hospital. 3. The road along the Rhine which Frost's battalion used to get to the Arnhem bridge.*

Top: *In war there is always paperwork: an open-air orderly room.*
Above right: *Arnhem, Onderlangs: Assault-gun 40-G (GIII SdKfz 142).*
Above: *Obergruppenführer Wilhelm Bittrich.*
Right: *The first PoWs are escorted to the Hartenstein Hotel's tennis court.*
Far right: *'Send everything to Arnhem!' (Hitler).*

Above left: *Arnhem, Utrecht road near Oranjestreet: After the battle.*
Above right: *Morning of 19 September 1944: When is the next lot coming?*
Right: *A few minutes' break.*
Far right: *With bag and baggage to Arnhem.*

48

Top: *England, 19 September 1944: The third wave.*
Above right: *Only about half of the 431 gliders reach their respective landing zones: A US Waco.*
Below right: *Horsa MkII*
Above: *A 2cm AA gun directly below the flight path.*
Centre: *AA gunners.*
Right: *Planes for Arnhem: when are they coming?*

Above: *US Waco after a nose-landing: German souvenir hunters.*
Right: *In the pilot's cabin of a Waco: a German paratrooper.*

The Third Day

19 September 1944

The official Allied summary

On Wednesday 20 September 1944 Allied Head-quarters reported on the events of the day before:

'Second Army near the Rhine — 53-mile advance across Holland — Armour closing on Nijmegen — Big new airborne force landed.

'The British Second Army has made a swift advance across Holland from the Belgian border, and advanced elements were last night three miles from Nijmegen, on the south bank of the Rhine, one of the areas where the Airborne Army had landed.

'General Dempsey's men advanced 53 miles in 48 hours. From Eindhoven, which has been captured by the Second Army, powerful armoured columns drove 37 miles on parallel routes, breaking through all opposition.

'Progress of the Airborne Army was described last night as excellent. As well as Nijmegen, the other main landing areas were Eindhoven and Arnhem, north of the Rhine. More strong forces were landed by air yesterday at unspecified points.

'The Germans say that more landings have been made in the province of Utrecht, nearer the coast . . .

'Latest reports reaching Supreme Allied Headquarters are that leading tanks have crossed the Maas River at Grave, eight miles south-west of Nijmegen, where airborne forces had captured the main road bridge across the river intact.

'It is officially stated that more strong formations of the Airborne Army landed in Holland yesterday; and there is reason to believe that they not only reinforced the troops already in position but invaded new territory.

German radio reports claim that the area south of the Zuider Zee is included.

'All the airborne forces in Holland have dug themselves into strong positions and beaten off all enemy attacks. Airborne Army Headquarters is in constant communication with all subordinate units, and the operations have so far followed the master plan without a hitch. Last night their progress was described by a staff officer as "excellent."

'Yesterday's 37-mile advance by Second Army columns, together with the 16-mile advance which brought them to Eindhoven on Monday, makes a 53-mile advance in 48 hours. At frequent points along their advance the columns joined with airborne groups holding open bridges and other vital junctions for the tanks.

'Along the route the British armour encountered German 88mm. anti-tank guns and Panther tanks dug into concrete emplacements, and groups of British tanks turned off from the columns to deal with these while the main body swept ahead. The tanks drove through and around Einhoven without stopping, leaving following units to mop up enemy resistance in the town. One tank column swerved four miles east of Eindhoven and took the main road through Geldrop, smashing strong resistance in that town and leaving it in the hands of following units.

'At Veghel, on a tributary of the Maas, the armoured columns met more airborne units in command of the bridge across the river and swept on 15 miles to Grave, where the Airborne Army was again in control. Before reaching Veghel a group of tanks covering the left flank of the main columns encountered the enemy at the town of Best and beat back German counter-attacks intended to interrupt the advance.

'It is confirmed that Eindhoven, Nijmegen, and Arnhem, on the northern branch of the Rhine delta, 10 miles from the frontier, are three of the main areas where the army landed on Sunday. The other landing zones are still unrevealed.

'The Germans facing the remainder of the Second Army north of the Escaut Canal are now virtually cut off by the drive towards the Rhine. That they are very strong forces is indicated by the successive counter-attacks they have been launching against our Escaut Canal bridgehead north of Gneel.' (*The Times*, London, 20.9.1944)

With the British 2nd Army

On 19 September 1944 the BBC in London carried this radio report from its man in Brussels:

'This is Frank Gillard, War Correspondent of the BBC, speaking from Brussels with a special despatch bringing good news of today's fighting in Holland. I want to thank listeners in Brussels, and I want to thank the radio authorities at this station for allowing me to break into your programme in this way, and to bring this despatch to you, because I'm sure you'll be interested in the news — it's good news — and also for letting me in this way bring the news to listeners in Great Britain and throughout the world.

'The British Second Army is off again. It has joined up with the airborne army near Eindhoven, and struck out for the Dutch Rhine. Yesterday afternoon just south of Eindhoven at the little village of Aalst there was some fierce fighting. The enemy made, or tried to make, one more stand. Our infantry stormed the German positions and turned the enemy out of concrete fortifications guarding the road, and then our tanks broke through. By seven o'clock our men were in Eindhoven from the south, and there they linked up with parachutists who fought their way in from the north round about midday. Earlier in the afternoon the Second Army Forces bypassing Eindhoven to the west had made an earlier junction with the airborne troops. Now the Second Army's armour pushed on to add its tremendous weight to the airborne strength already landed farther north. On the Wilhelmina Canal they were held up by a demolished bridge, but sappers worked right through the night, last night, and by 5.30 this morning a new bridge was open. The Second Army streamed over and a most amazing advance began. It was an express drive right across Holland, linking up all the way with parachutists and airborne forces who prepared the ground and made the advance possible by seizing the bridges and the road junctions. In five hours — five hours only — an advance of almost 30 miles had been made, and our armoured columns had reached a point only three miles from Nijmegen on the banks of the Waal River, one of the

BRITISH ARMOUR REACHES AIRBORNE TROOPS

◆

REINFORCEMENTS POURED INTO HOLLAND

SECOND ARMY BEYOND EINDHOVEN

A BOULOGNE FORTRESS FALLS TO CANADIANS

Airborne troops and supplies were still being poured into Holland yesterday, and the First Airborne Army has gained its initial objectives and taken prisoners.

The first advanced armoured patrols of the British Second Army driving north from the Belgian border have established contact with the airborne forces. The Second Army, by-passing Eindhoven, has advanced 15 miles in just over 24 hours.

In the fight for Boulogne the fortress of Mont Lambert surrendered yesterday to the Canadians, who now hold most of the town east of the river. On the American Third Army front General Patton's tanks are 18 miles beyond Nancy.

Above left: *Excerpt from* The Times *of 19 September 1944.*
Above right: *19 September 1944: bitter fighting between the railway line and the Lower Rhine.*

lower stretches of the Rhine, and they were only seven miles from Germany itself.

'It's an incredible achievement; certainly one of the outstanding operations of the whole war. And now what is the result? The result is that the airborne and the Second Army troops between them have cut the whole of Holland south of the Rhine clean in two. Once we reach Nijmegen every German west of our new position will have to fight his way through our lines to get back to Germany, or somehow get across the river to the north. That's the immediate result of this amazing thirty-mile dash. More may follow, for the momentum of General Dempsey's troops, both the old stagers of the Second Army and the airborne newcomers, is by no means expended yet.'

Situation at 23.59 hours on 19 Sept. 1944

Div. HQ

HQ of Airlanding Brigade

HQ of Parachute Brigade

Company

Battalion

Wolfhezen

Johanna Hoeve

Lichtenbeek

10th Battalion, 4th Parachute Brigade
156th Battalion, 4th Parachute Brigade
21st Independent Parachute Company
Battalion, Glider Pilots Regiment

7th Battalion King's Own
Scottish Borderers

Units of
2nd Battalion South Staffordshire Reg
1st Battalion, 1st Parachute Brig
3rd Battalion, 1st Parachute Brig
11th Battalion, 4th Parachute Brig

1st Brit Airborne Division HQ

Battalion, Glider Pilots Reg

ARNHEM

St. Elisabeth's Hospital

Heelsum

Den Brink

Renkum

1st Company Border Regiment
1st Light Regiment, Royal Artillery

Heveadorp

Ferry Oosterbeek

Pontoonbridge

2nd Bat 1st Parachute Brig

Westerbouwing

Bridge

3rd Comp

1st Parachute Brig

Lower Rhine

Railway
Bridge

Heteren

Driel

Elden

0   ½   1   2 Miles

55

The official German summary

This communiqué summarising the previous day was issued by the German High Command on 20 September:

'In Central Holland enemy airborne forces in the Arnhem area were further compressed by our concentrated attacks. Supported by Luftwaffe fighter-bombers our troops inflicted heavy losses of men and equipment. More than 1700 prisoners have been taken so far. In the Eindhoven area enemy tanks have advanced in a north-easterly direction, and our forces have launched a counter-attack. North-west of Aix-la-Chapelle the enemy has been able to extend his bridgehead by deploying great numbers of tanks. North-east of the town all enemy attacks have been repulsed with heavy losses to the enemy. Fierce fighting is continuing in the Nancy-Luneville area. Nancy has fallen to the enemy but the fighting continues in Luneville. Minor actions only are reported on all other sectors of the front.'

The course of the battle

In Urquhart's absence the Headquarters of the 1st Airborne Division had been established in Oosterbeek's Hartenstein Hotel. There, in the cellar taking refuge from the German bombardment, Brigadiers Hackett and Hicks were at odds over command of the division; Hicks had already assumed command, but Hackett was the senior in rank.

At first light, 04.00hrs, on 19 September, Lea's 11th Parachute Bn and McCardie's 2nd Bn South Staffords tried to resume their advance through the network of streets between the Arnhem museum and the St Elizabeth Hospital. But lacking adequate anti-tank weapons and artillery support the British were soon beaten back. The failure did have a beneficial side-effect, though, because the South Staffords, retiring to form a defensive line at the Rhine Pavillion, forced the self-propelled gun parked in Zwarteweg to move as they made their way back. This allowed General Urquhart, who had been living for two days on nothing but candy, to leave the attic where he had been sheltering.

So, at exactly 07.15hrs on 19 September, Urquhart, the man nobody had expected to see again, materialised at the Headquarters of the British First Airborne Division. One of his first actions was to try and establish the long overdue coordination of an assault by the 11th Parachute Bn and 2nd South Staffords. Colonel Barlow, Hick's Deputy, was sent forward to set this up, but he never made it; he was subsequently reported missing and his body was never found.

Meanwhile, Frost's battalion was still fighting desperately at the bridge, where the Germans were throwing more and more troops to the battle. At the same time the ring the Germans had thrown round the rest of the division was tightening. Throughout the whole of Tuesday morning and part of the afternoon the 10th Parachute Bn, holding the northern flank of Hackett's sector of the perimeter, was subjected to heavy fire from mortars, tanks and artillery. The 18 houses originally

Below: *Major-General Robert E. Urquhart in front of the Hartenstein Hotel.*
Above right: *Oosterbeek: a British 75mm howitzer in action.*
Bottom: *German prisoners cooking a meal in the grounds of the Hartenstein Hotel.*
Below right: *2cm AA gun at the corner of Johan de Witt Street and Heuvelink Boulevard, Arnhem.*

occupied by Frost's men had been reduced to 10 and eventually no more than 200 paratroops were holding out in the vicinity of the bridge, putting up a spirited resistance from positions that were proof against the murderous German fire. Their food had run out and their water supply was cut off, so they were reduced to living on whatever they could scavenge from the houses they were occupying. The Germans tried to persuade Frost to surrender, but he refused, so Brigadeführer Harmel ordered his gunners and tank commanders systematically to destroy every house still in British hands. 'If the British won't come out,' he told his officers, 'we'll have to fumigate their holes. From now on, shoot every house to pieces from ground-floor to attic. Don't leave a stone standing.'

The meteorological experts had forecast a cloudless sky that afternoon, but the weather had steadily deteriorated since the morning. Low clouds shrouded the southern air lane over the Channel, so that the third phase of Operation Market Garden had barely begun before it ran into difficulty. Some glider pilots unable to keep their towing aircraft in sight had to cast off prematurely and make emergency landings in England or go down in the Channel. Whole groups of transport aircraft were compelled to turn back and fighter squadrons, unable to locate their targets in the thick fog, had to return with their missions unaccomplished. Fewer than half the 655 troop-carrying aircraft and 431 gliders reached the landing zones. Urquhart had been counting on reinforcement by the Polish Parachute Brigade, whose lift was scheduled for Tuesday, 19 September, but the adverse weather enforced a postponement of their drop.

There was another setback when 163 supply aircraft deposited their cargoes on a pre-arranged landing zone that had fallen into enemy hands. The frustrated men surrounded in Oosterbeek did everything they could think of to attract the aircrews' attention but to no avail; the pilots and despatchers stuck manfully to their orders. They did not know the Germans had a trump card. On the first day of the operation they had captured a British officer carrying a set of instructions for marking out the supply dropping zones and the procedure for signalling with smoke and Verey lights. Consequently, the Germans not only knew just where the supplies would be dropped, but also how to direct the supply aircraft right to the spot. The airborne troops' disappointment was only aggravated by the aircrews' unshakeable determination to execute their orders as they flew steadily through deadly flak which inflicted heavy losses. The exhausted soldiers had to watch helplessly as a squadron of 35 Stirling bombers dropped their containers on enemy ground. Only about half of the 87 tons of ammunition and supplies destined for the Airborne Division that day actually reached the troops in the perimeter.

In this crisis the airborne troops had allies to hand who might have influenced events quickly and decisively: the gallant, well-disciplined and comparatively well-

Above left: *Arnhem: AA gunners at the corner of Johan de Witt Street and Heuvelink Boulevard.*
Above right: *The operation has failed: en route to the PoW camp.*
Below centre: *At Velperplein.*
Below right: *Nachtegaalpad (the 'nightingales' path').*

equipped Dutch Resistance. One group was actually awaiting orders to go to the aid of Colonel Frost's sorely tried paratroops at the Arnhem bridge. 'But nobody wanted us', members of the Resistance complained afterwards. It seems quite likely that the British airborne commanders were secretly instructed not to let members of the Dutch Resistance get involved in the fighting. A different approach was adopted by the 101st and 82nd US Division; Generals Taylor and Gavin were quick to lift any restrictions on providing Dutch Resistance fighters with arms and equipment, and Dutchmen were soon fighting alongside the Americans.

As no news was coming out of the Arnhem area through official channels the headquarters of the 82nd US Airborne Division got its first indication of the 1st Airborne Division's desperate situation from a Dutchman's telephone call. The British in Arnhem, he

told them were in danger of being wiped out by German panzers.

On 19 September the weather deteriorated to such an extent that paratroop drops were totally impossible. German counter-attacks launched from the Reichswald on the Groesbeek were repulsed with great difficulty, and by the evening, the Guards Armoured Division had managed to link up with the 82nd Airborne Division at Nijmegen. The Allied ground forces had now covered two-thirds of the distance to Arnhem, but they still had the Waal to cross and 500 men of the Waffen SS were holding the bridge across it. An attempt to outflank the bridge by taking a route through the Huner Park between the bridge and Nijmegen that day was thwarted; a fresh effort was anticipated next day.

Meantime Henri Knap, the head of the Dutch Resistance Intelligence Service in the Arnhem area, had been told by two of his agents that a Panzer regiment with Tiger tanks was driving towards Oosterbeek and Arnhem. He decided to warn the British. Despite the risks of using the telephone, he got through to the headquarters of the Airborne Division, only to be told to hang on while his message was passed on to an officer. Several whole minutes elapsed. At length the HQ telephone was picked up again and Knap was told that 'The captain doesn't think your information is correct. He's already heard too many rumours of that sort.'

Still nobody in Britain knew what was really happening in Arnhem, as radio contact with the British 1st Airborne Division was non-existent. The paratroops, it was thought, were holding on firmly to the northern access to the bridge. Not even in Eisenhower's headquarters was anyone aware of the seriousness of the situation; certainly no hint of a crisis emerged from official statements issued at this time — indeed the overall impression was that everything had gone according to plan. Browning himself had no idea that by now Urquhart's airborne troops were battling against two Panzer divisions.

To summarise, then, 19 September was a turning point. The three battalions which had tried to get through to Frost had been decimated; the supply drops had gone astray; and the expected Polish Parachute Brigade had failed to arrive.

Above right: *Arnhem Onderlangs: aftermath of the battle in the centre of the town.*
Below right: *Arnhem: In England they have no idea ...*
Far right: *Arnhem, Utrecht Street: British dead.*

Top and below left: *The 2nd British Army has established an armoured corridor: Sherman tanks on the march.*
Above: *War correspondent Sergeant Lewis.*

The Fourth Day

20 September 1944

The official Allied summary

On Thursday 21 September Allied Headquarters reported the events of the previous day as follows:

'British reach the Rhine — Fierce struggle for bridge at Nijmegen — Poles establish new front on the Scheldt — Capture of Boulogne.

'Armoured forces of the British Second Army last night reached the south bank of the River Waal (the Dutch name for the Rhine) at Nijmegen...

'The armoured corridor established through Holland is being attacked on the flanks, but our forces are being built up in the area round Nijmegen.

'Polish troops of the Canadian Army have reached the Scheldt on a six-mile front.

'It was reported late last night that the town of Boulogne is now in our hands, but still under fire from Germans in the hills...

'The battle of Holland is raging furiously at many points, and is at its fiercest at Nijmegen, a few miles from the German frontier, and at Arnhem, about 10 miles north of Nijmegen.

'At Arnhem the allied airborne troops have not yet been relieved by the British Second Army, whose leading tank formations were reported last night to be fighting for the bridge at Nijmegen.

'The British Second Army has established an armoured corridor through Holland to the banks of the Waal at Nijmegen. The base of this corridor has been extended to Duizel and Wilreit, about 10 miles south-west of Eindhoven, and this, with the inclusion of Geldrop, east of Eindhoven, gives the corridor a width of about 15 miles at its greatest.

'In spite of bad weather more supplies were flown in yesterday to the airborne army, who are fighting well and retain the initiative. No enemy counter-attack has yet driven them from their positions, nor has the enemy been able to raise anything like a major counter-offensive against those gained jointly be the airborne army and General Dempsey's tank columns.

'Airborne and armoured units have been disposed all along both flanks of the corridor to defend it against strong German counter-attacks which have been launched with the aim of cutting through.

'The British Second Army forces west of the corridor have started to come up. They have advanced northward from their Escaut Canal bridgehead north of Lommel to Grootbosch, three or four miles inside Holland. They are pushing ahead of them a German force estimated to be 100,000 strong.

'The weather, after favouring us for the first two days of the battle of Holland, changed yesterday in the enemy's favour, as it did in Normandy. There was heavy rain, ground haze and low cloud over Holland, so that it is unlikely that airborne reinforcements in any great strength were flown into the battle yesterday.' (*The Times*, London, 21.9.1944)

The official German summary

On 21 September 1944 the German High Command reported:

'In Central Holland most of the Airborne Division which landed in the Arnhem region has been destroyed despite reinforcements being sent in by air. What now remains of the division has been compressed into a small area and 2800 prisoners, including the Divisional Commander [This reported capture of a 'Divisional Commander' in the Arnhem area — supposedly Urquhart — was fiction] have been taken to date. Near Nijmegen our forces are locked in a fierce battle with enemy armour attacking from the direction of Eindhoven. South of the mouth of the Scheldt the enemy has succeeded in penetrating our lines at some points. Yesterday in the Aachen region powerful enemy attacks were repulsed and a counter attack north-east of the town has succeeded in restoring our front. In three days 47 enemy tanks have been destroyed in the fighting in this sector of the front alone.

In several days' fighting an enemy force which crossed the Sauer, north-east of Echternach, has also been virtually wiped out.'

In the late evening of 21 September Radio Berlin read out another communiqué issued by the German High Command: 'In the Arnhem area the operations of the British 1st Airborne Division have been hampered by demolished bridges. The fighting between Eindhoven and Nijmegen appears to have reached its peak, and in Nijmegen a fierce house-to-house and street battle has developed, with the airborne troops putting up a desperate resistance in the hope of relief by the British Second Army coming from Eindhoven.'

The course of the battle
On the morning of 20 September the Polish General Sosabowski was advised of a change of plan. A new dropping zone for his Polish Parachute Brigade had been chosen near Driel, several kilometres west of the original site close to Elden, at the southern approach to the Arnhem bridge. Not only had Sosabowski briefed his men on the basis of the Elden DZ plan, but he was only told of the revised scheme three hours before his men were due to emplane. That, plus the fact that their operation had been postponed several times in the previous 48 hours did not get the operation off to an orderly start. Fresh operational orders were hurriedly issued, however, Sosabowski and his men duly emplaned and the aircraft were set to take off. Then yet again, the drop was deferred because of bad weather.

Within the Oosterbeek perimeter near the Hartenstein Hotel, more than 72 hours after the first landings, the Airborne Division was now preparing for the battle which would seal its fate. The four battalions which had striven to fight their way through to the bridge had virtually ceased to exist. The survivors of Frost's badly battered 2nd Parachute Battalion were still holding out near the bridge, 4 miles east of the perimeter, but Hackett's 4th Parachute Brigade had suffered heavy casualties in a withdrawal to the perimeter, around which the Germans were welding a ring of steel.

At the bridge itself, that Wednesday evening passed off comparatively quietly. Frost sent out patrols to check that there was no way of breaking out of his encircled

Top: *Excerpt from* The Times *of 20.9.1944.*
Above: *Polish Paratroops waiting to emplane.*
Right: *The Arnhem road bridge: Captain Gräbner's reconnaissance unit has been shot to pieces on the road.*

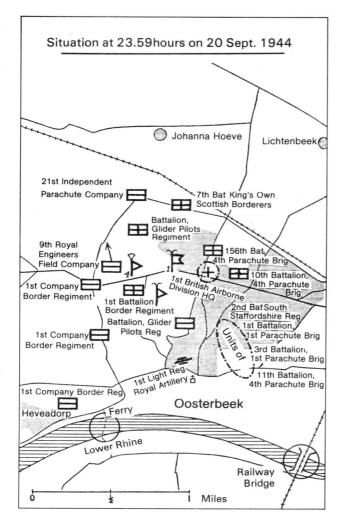

Situation at 23.59 hours on 20 Sept. 1944

Johanna Hoeve

Lichtenbeek

21st Independent
Parachute Company

7th Bat King's Own
Scottish Borderers

Battalion,
Glider Pilots
Regiment

9th Royal
Engineers
Field Company

156th Bat,
4th Parachute Brig

10th Battalion,
4th Parachute
Brig

1st British Airborne
Division HQ

1st Company
Border Regiment

1st Battalion
Border Regiment

2nd Bat South
Staffordshire Reg

Battalion, Glider
Pilots Reg

1st Battalion,
1st Parachute Brig

1st Company
Border Regiment

Units of

3rd Battalion,
1st Parachute Brig

11th Battalion,
4th Parachute Brig

1st Light Reg
Royal Artillery

1st Company Border Reg

Heveadorp

Ferry

Oosterbeek

Lower Rhine

Railway
Bridge

0   ½   1   Miles

position; there was none. After dark the burning
buildings turned night into day and the fighting
intensified. At dawn the Luftwaffe joined in, and while
strafing and bombing the houses occupied by the
paratroops one Me109 flew into a church steeple and
burst into flames. Grimly the British clung on,
surrounded on three side by blazing houses and almost
out of ammunition. By this time only a handful of Frost's
men were left standing and those capable of walking split
up into little groups to try and make a fighting
withdrawal from the town. They had little idea that the
rest of the Division in the perimeter was also in desperate
straits, or that their only hope of survival lay in the
advance of the British XXXth Corps from the south.
The 1st Airborne Division had been expected to hold the
bridge for 24 hours only, after which the XXXth Corps
would have come to the relief of the paratroops in
Arnhem. In the event Frost's 2nd Parachute Battalion
was the only unit in the whole Airborne Division to
reach the objective, but it managed to hold out three
times as long as planned.

Moreover, because of Frost's stubborn stand at the

Above left: *Nijmegen: the bridge that was so tenaciously defended.*
Below: *After the battle: a priest with a seriously wounded German soldier.*
Below left: *British Cromwell tank: no orders to advance.*
Bottom: *British sapper, German explosives: the bridge is intact in British hands.*

bridge the IInd SS-Panzer Corps was unable to exert any influence on the battle around Nijmegen. Harmel's 10th SS-Panzer Division could not cross the Arnhem bridge and get to Nijmegen, and the bridge was barred to other vehicles carrying reinforcements to the German troops who were resisting the advance of the Guards Armoured Division towards Arnhem.

Radio communication within the Airborne Division had now broken down completely. Nobody, it seemed, wanted to know that the two public telephone networks in Gelderland were unscathed and usable. 'We can manage with our own wireless equipment', one British officer is said to have retorted when a member of the Dutch underground tried to persuade him to use the public telephone. In fairness, one must add that the Arnhem telephone exchange was under German control and almost all private lines had been cut; but the leaders of the local underground groups had secretly arranged for trustworthy and reliable operators to man the exchange. Mention must also be made of the existence of a private telephone service connecting the power stations in the Gelderland region (known as the PGEM). Every power station in the province had a telephone on this net, enabling them to speak not only to other stations in the province but to any other station throughout Holland. Moreover, by dialling a particular code on this system it was possible to cut in on the public telephone network.

The Germans recognised the value of the Dutch telephone installations and did not hesitate to make use of them. The war diary of the Hohenstaufen Division reported that 'the existence of a first-class telephone service in Holland was a tremendous advantage at Arnhem. We had only a few wireless sets that would work during this phase of the operations, and the Dutch telephone network enabled us to dispense with radio communication.'

Around noon on 20 September a message was handed to General Browning. For the first time since the operation began it gave him a realistic picture of the situation at Arnhem. 'Some of our troops are still holding the northern approaches of the bridge,' it ran, 'but we have no contact with them and cannot reinforce or re-supply them...the whole of Arnhem is in enemy hands...relief urgently requested...a fierce battle is raging and the enemy attacking with determination...the outlook is serious...'

The road bridge north of Nijmegen was captured intact by American airborne forces at 19.15hrs on 20 September and crossed by a British armoured column from the XXXth Corps.

The men of the Waffen SS who were holding the bridge were all killed during the action. According to Dutch sources the bridge was saved because a young member of the Dutch Resistance, Jan van Hoof, regardless of a hail of bullets cut the wires connected to the explosive charges which had been placed in the girders. The British were now less than 10 miles from Arnhem, but the impetus of the attack seemed to have

Below: *In the perimeter: supplies are hard to come by.*
Above right: *Oosterbeek: one of Lt-Colonel Harzer's tanks with a British parachute in the foreground.*
Bottom: *Oosterbeek: first interrogation.*
Below right: *Arnhem: German assault gun at the corner of Nieuwe and Roermonds place — 'not a happy situation'.*

petered out. Major Trotter, the British officer commanding the armoured column, astonished the Americans when he told them he had been ordered not to push on, and that anyway the tanks could not advance without an infantry escort. So the armour settled down for the night.

Actually the Allies could thank Fieldmarshal Model for their capture of the strategically important Nijmegen bridge intact. Model had stubbornly and repeatedly refused to order its demolition, despite the pleas of General Christiansen, the military commander of the Netherlands. The latter wanted this bridge to be taken out at the very beginning of Operation Market Garden, but Model was more concerned to hold it.

Although the Allies had reached Nijmegen and even captured the bridge over the Waal, the battle at Arnhem had already been lost. Lifts of reinforcements for the hard-pressed airborne troops, which were to have been flown in on the second and third days, had been cancelled. At first the planes could not take off from their bases in Britain because of fog; then, when the weather improved, they ran into murderous anti-aircraft fire, which slaughtered hundreds of men on their parachutes or in their gliders. Supplies and ammunition intended for the beleaguered Airborne Division were dropped in areas held by the Germans — although, according to operational plans, no Germans were supposed to be there. Meantime enemy reinforcements were being rushed up from Germany, amongst them units of General von Zangen's Fifteenth Army, which by Montgomery's reckoning were all trapped around Antwerp.

But as yet few experienced troops and battle-tried formations were available in the immediate battle area and this hampered the Germans' plans to counter the airborne invasion. A miscellaneous collection of units and inexperienced troops had to be committed to the battle, adding to the difficulty of coordinating the counter-measures; shortages of ammunition were a further handicap. However, newly raised commando units proved a decisive factor in the outcome of the battle, by identifying the dropping zones, assessing their relative importance and launching immediate assaults on them.

Above left: *Oosterbeek, Utrecht Street: a 40-G assault gun and British PoWs.*
Above right: *Arnhem, near the museum on Utrecht Street: incessant assaults.*
Centre and below left: *Oosterbeek, Vreewijk Hotel: murderous defensive fire.*
Left: *Arnhem: the 'Red Devils' got as far as this.*

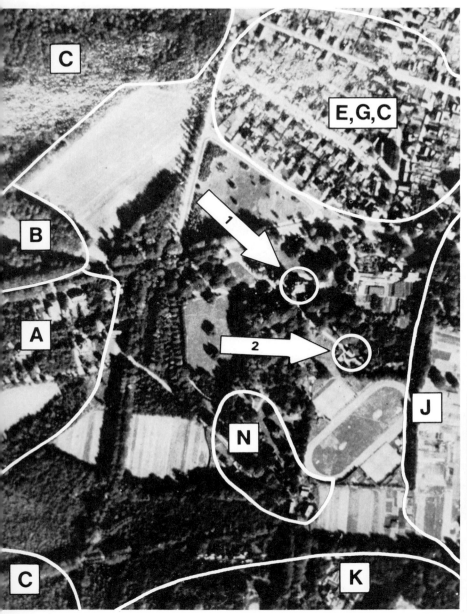

Above left: *The Oosterbeek perimeter: 1. Hartenstein Hotel, HQ of Urquhart's 1st Airborne Division. 2. HQ Brigadier J. W. Hackett's 4th Parachute Brigade. A. Bn Glider Pilots Regiment. B. 9th Field Coy RE. C. Coy of 1st Bn Border Rgt. E. 7th Bn KOSB. G. 21 Indep Para Coy. K. Lonsdale Group (a composite unit consisting of the survivors of the 1st and 3rd Staffords and the 11th Bn Parachute Regt under command of Major Dickie Londsdale, the former 2 i/c of the 11th Bn). J. 10th Para Bn. N Bn Glider Pilots Regt.*

Above right and lower centre: *There were German troops where none were supposed to be.*

Far right: *Arnhem: Nieuwe Kran in the foreground, with Nieuwe Plein and Rijnstraat behind: plenty of action.*

Top: *Inside the perimeter at the Hartenstein Hotel: preparing for the last stand with revolver and folding knife.*
Above right: *British 75mm field gun.*
Above: *'Red Devil' J. Connington of Selby, Yorkshire, with his Sten.*
Right: *Heaven-sent supplies.*
Far right: *'Red Devils'.*

Top: *Oosterbeek perimeter, 'Red Devils': 'relief is needed'.*
Top: *Wolfheze: outposts on the Duitsekampweg.*
Below right: *Arnhem: the evacuation of a hospital on Velperplein.*

The Fifth Day

21 September 1944

The Official Allied summary

On Friday 22 September, Allied Headquarters issued this communiqué on the events of the previous day:

'British tanks driving on to Arnhem — Enemy shelled by Second Army's guns — Relief for airborne force imminent — Aachen in ring of battles.

'British tanks have crossed the Waal at Nijmegen and are driving northward to link up with the hard-pressed airborne force at Arnhem, on the Lek. Medium artillery of the Second Army was reported early to-day to be shelling targets indicated by the Arnhem force, whose relief is now regarded as imminent . . .

'General Dempsey's tanks and allied paratroops were fighting their way last night through strong German forces to reach the hard-pressed airborne troops at Arnhem, whose relief, after holding off heavy and repeated attacks for four days, is imminent.

'It is officially confirmed that the vital bridge over the Waal (the southern branch of the lower Rhine) has been captured intact by a pincer movement, the American airborne troops swinging in from the north-west simultaneously with a British attack from the south. Although the bridge had been prepared for demolition, it had not been blown, probably because there were large German forces still fighting on the other side.

'In Nijmegen itself fierce fighting is still in progress, with the Germans using tanks. The battle for the bridge has been won, but the struggle for the town is by no means over. Generally, the news from this sector has improved, but there is much hard fighting ahead.

'Polish airborne troops were reported last night to

have been dropped as reinforcements in Holland — at what points was not stated, but it is quite possible that they have been landed at Arnhem. It was announced that the Arnhem forces had received more supplies from aircraft yesterday. The machines flew through unfavourable weather, which restricted cover, and although they succeeded in their mission some losses were reported.

'Strong groups of the 70,000 Germans cut off by the allied northward thrust from the Dutch border are trying to break through to the German border by using tanks against the screen protecting the flanks of the 40-mile-long corridor. All these attacks are being rolled back, and the allies are broadening the corridor while supplies and men are rushed northwards to fight in the Rhine battles. The Germans are using fairly large numbers of tanks — not too skilfully — as there was a tank training section in this part of Holland . . .

'A staff officer in the battle area described them as "keen but ineffective." This remark seems to fit most of the German troops between our corridor and the sea.

'The weather was again bad over Holland, and a fair number of enemy fighters came up to attack the airborne reinforcements. In a battle near Nijmegen Thunderbolts shot down 20 German fighters for the loss of four of their own machines.' (*The Times,* London, 22.9.1944)

The Official German summary

The German High Command reported thus on the events of 22 September:

'In the Arnhem area our troops continued their efforts

to wipe out the remnants of the British 1st Airborne Division, and the enemy advance northwards from Nijmegen has been checked; south of Arnhem we are slowly gaining ground. Luftwaffe fighters and fighter bomber aircraft are supporting our ground forces fighting in Holland, and they have already destroyed more than 38 enemy planes, including 20 of the enemy's supply dropping transports and 12 big four-engined bombers. Ten Anglo-American bombers are also reported to have been shot down by anti-aircraft fire. In the Aachen region several enemy attacks have been repulsed and nine enemy tanks have been destroyed. Enemy pressure south-east of the town is increasing.

The course of the battle

During Wednesday night a reconnaissance patrol of eleven airborne Sappers was sent out from the perimeter to reconnoitre a route to the cable ferry linking Heveadorp and Driel. They knew where the ferry was supposed to be operating, but the could find no trace of it. They returned to the perimeter with the impression that the German had removed the ferry but in fact it had been beached, undamaged and quite serviceable, near the demolished railway bridge, only a mile west of its normal crossing point.

Meanwhile the Polish Parachute Brigade had been given fresh orders. Sosabowski's men were still to be flown in to reinforce the well-nigh exhausted 'Red Devils', but were now to reach them by way of the ferry. Urquhart, still ignorant of the state of Frost's battalion, was also unaware that the ferry had not been located. At 09.00hrs he wirelessed a message to Browning that the enemy was putting his full weight into attacks on the bridge, making the defenders' situation critical; the Germans were also attacking Heelsum and the British positions west of Arnhem, creating a serious situation in both areas. Urquhart went on to say that he was taking up an all-round defensive position based on the Hartenstein with the rest of the division, and that relief in both sectors had become imperative. The Heveadorp ferry, he affirmed, was still in British hands.

Urquhart's reports were relayed to XXX Corps, and from them Horrocks deduced that both the bridge and the Driel terminal of the ferry were held by the British. Consequently he told the commander of the Guards Armoured Division, whose orders were to advance to the Arnhem bridge up the main Nijmegen-Arnhem Road, that should he find the main road blocked, he should try the road to the Driel ferry. To secure that end of the ferry the Polish Parachute Brigade would be dropped near Driel during the afternoon. When the two forces had linked up, the Poles and the Guards Armoured Division would together establish a base from which infantry could be ferried across the Rhine to relieve Urquhart.

Even as Horrocks was actually issuing his orders the last of Frost's positions near the bridge were being overwhelmed and an important topographical feature on the north bank of the Lower Rhine near Westerbouwing,

BRITISH REACH THE RHINE

FIERCE STRUGGLE FOR BRIDGE AT NIJMEGEN

POLES ESTABLISH NEW FRONT ON THE SCHELDT

CAPTURE OF BOULOGNE

Armoured forces of the British Second Army last night reached the south bank of the River Waal (the Dutch name for the Rhine) at Nijmegen.

The armoured corridor established through Holland is being attacked on the flanks, but our forces are being built up in the area round Nijmegen.

Polish troops of the Canadian Army have reached the Scheldt on a six-mile front.

It was reported late last night that the town of Boulogne is now in our hands, but still under fire from Germans in the hills.

Above left: *Excerpt from* The Times *of 21.9.1944.*
Above right: *After waiting for three days, Polish paratroops emplane.*
Far left: *Arnhem bridge.*
Left: *SS-Panzer Division: a pause in the battle.*

dominating the Driel ferry terminal, had just been seized by the Germans. Since dawn on Thursday 21 September the battle for the Arnhem bridge had entered its final phase; half of Frost's force had been killed or wounded and the majority of the survivors were captured during the course of the morning. Only a few escaped with the help of members of the Dutch Resistance. The British wounded were astonished by and decidedly wary of the attitude of their SS captors, who jovially handed out cigarettes, chocolate and brandy. Bitterly the paratroops recognised the cigarettes and chocolate as British-made and thus in all probability part of the air supplies which had been intended for the Airborne Division anyway. Bittrich, the commander of II SS-Panzer Korps, said later it was 'a matter of chivalry' to show due respect to his adversaries in the Arnhem-Nijmegen fighting. 'These men', he said, 'were tough, well-trained soldiers — typically British — whom we had been fighting since D-Day. Their morale was superb. The troops at the

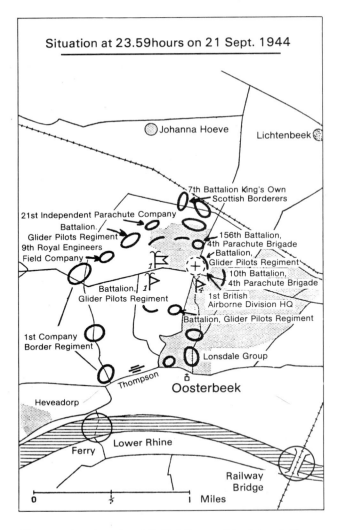

Situation at 23.59hours on 21 Sept. 1944

Johanna Hoeve

Lichtenbeek

7th Battalion King's Own
Scottish Borderers

21st Independent Parachute Company

Battalion,
Glider Pilots Regiment

9th Royal Engineers
Field Company

156th Battalion,
4th Parachute Brigade

Battalion,
Glider Pilots Regiment

10th Battalion,
4th Parachute Brigade

1st British
Airborne Division HQ

Battalion,
Glider Pilots Regiment

Battalion, Glider Pilots Regiment

1st Company
Border Regiment

Lonsdale Group

Thompson

Oosterbeek

Heveadorp

Ferry

Lower Rhine

Railway
Bridge

0   ½   1   Miles

Above centre: *A captured British 6-pr anti-tank gun in the Arnhem area.*
Above right: *German infantry evacuating casualties near Onderlangs-Bovenover.*
Right: *Oosterbeek: An improvised AA post.*
Far right: *Nijmegen — Arnhem: a Jagdpanther tank destroyer and a Dakota.*

Arnhem bridge fought a hard and gallant battle, and at the end of it their morale was still high.'

Early on Thurday morning the Germans managed to clear away the debris blocking access to the bridge and open a narrow passage for vehicles. As soon as organised resistance by the paratroops at the bridge had ended, Bittrich ordered Harzer, the commander of the Hohenstaufen Division, to destroy the remainder of the Airborne Division dug in at Oosterbeek before the British Second Army could reach the southern bank of the river.

Back on the XXX Corps front, at 10.40hrs the Irish Guards of the Guards Armoured Division had been ordered to resume their advance. They were given only 20 minutes to get ready to cross the start line outside Nijmegen at 11.00hrs, then make for Arnhem. There was little time to check equipment; maps were scarce and information scanty on the placing of the Germans' deadly 8.8cm AA guns which had been set up as anti-tank weapons. After a quick study of some captured sketches, the commander of the vanguard, Captain Langton, led the column away.

Nervewracking days of waiting ended for the Polish Parachute Brigade, which took off at 14.15 in atrocious weather, with dense low clouds limiting visibility, the Dakotas climbed to 10,000ft and were above the clouds when a radio message suddenly ordered them to return to base. But only about half the aircraft heard the order and turned back. The rest continued on course to Holland, and three hours later, at 17.15hrs, approached the dropping zone through a curtain of deadly flak from weapons of virtually every calibre. Small arms fire took a heavy toll of the paratroops as they dropped and those who did land safely found themselves in the middle of the battle for Oosterbeek, caught between British and German fire. The Polish Brigade was only at half-strength before it suffered its first losses, as apart from the results of the misunderstanding while it was in flight, its glider-borne anti-tank unit had been air-landed on the far side of the Rhine during the second day (19 September) and had joined the 1st Airborne Division at Oosterbeek.

The surviving Polish paratroops assembled and moved towards the ferry terminal, whence their orders were to cross the river to the aid of the sorely-pressed 'Red Devils'. But there was no sign of any ferry, nor any other visible means of crossing the 400 metres-wide waterway. Moreover, any movement along the south bank promptly drew the fire of the German machine-guns on the other side. There was no sign of life from Oosterbeek and despite repeated attempts radio contact could not be established with the 1st Airborne Division.

Unwittingly, the Poles now settled the fate of the 1st Airborne Division. When Obergruppenführer Bittrich saw them floating down, it did not occur to him that they had been sent to reinforce Urquhart's perimeter; he assumed that they had been dropped to block the route from Arnhem to Nijmegen along which the 10th SS-Panzer Division was now moving, so he pulled the Knaust combat group out of the fighting around Oosterbeek and ordered it into the Elst area. Knaust's group, which was equipped with 20 Tiger and 20 Panther tanks, was told to stop the Poles from linking up with Horrocks' armoured column and getting control of the southern approaches to the Arnhem bridge. At the same time the 10th SS-Panzer Division was directed to advance to the Waal in order to check the British advance from Nijmegen towards Arnhem.

Bittrich's intention was above all to stop Horrocks

Below: *Trenches in the Oosterbeek perimeter.*
Above right: *British 6-pr anti-tank gun in action.*
Below right: *A jeep in flames.*

82

from reaching Arnhem and that consequently doomed Urquhart's Oosterbeek bridgehead. Unaware of this latest development, Horrocks signalled Urquhart that the 43rd Division had been ordered to relieve him that day, regardless of cost, that it was already approaching the ferry and that, if the situation permitted, it would cross immediately. Urquhart radioed back that the 43rd would be sure of a warm welcome.

By this time the British 1st Airborne Division had almost ceased to exist. Ammunition, medical dressings and water were in short supply. The edges of the perimeter were steadily being eroded until it now encompassed a zone along the Lower Rhine resembling a finger tip about 2 miles long and 1500 yds wide. Under constant attack from three sides on the ground and from the air, the division was being systematically destroyed platoon by platoon. Close support could be provided only by the RAF and the ground commanders were anxious for its fighters and bombers to blast a passage for the relief force, and at the same time to ease the pressure on Urquhart's men. The area around Oosterbeek was crowded with German artillery positions and swarming with vehicles. Urquhart repeatedly urged Browning to let the RAF bomb and strafe at will, but the airmen demanded precise information on the location of targets before they would attack; they wanted the Oosterbeek pocket to be defined by a bombline, which was impossible, so the Germans were left undisturbed.

Approximately 1500 men of the Polish Parachute Brigade had dropped near Driel, but when they concentrated at last light only about 750 were still alive and many of the survivors were wounded. Unable to cross the river to join the British in Oosterbeek, they formed a defensive area at Driel. At 21.00hrs Sosabowski heard from Urquhart. As there was no radio communication between the Airborne Division and the Poles, Captain Zwolanski, the Polish liaison officer with the Airborne Division, had to swim the Rhine to tell Sosabowski that Urquhart expected the Poles to cross the river that night. Urquhart said he was arranging rafts, but when immediately Sosabowski sent men down to the river bank there was no sign of them. Nor did any appear during the next few hours, so at 03.00hrs Sosabowski decided something had gone wrong and pulled his men back to their defensive position. Not a single Pole crossed the river that night.

Top: *The battle for the perimeter: 'What do we do next?'*
Above right: *Hartenstein Hotel: picking off snipers with a US MI carbine.*
Centre: *A 'Red Devil'.*
Right: *Laying out a ground recognition panel.*
Far right: *A supply container.*

Above: *Arnhem Bridge: on Thursday morning the Germans succeed in clearing the wreckage from the road.*
Right: *The 'Red Devils': two of the survivors.*

86

The Sixth Day

22 September 1944

The official Allied summary

The communiqué issued by Allied Headquarters on Saturday 23 September read as follows:

'Tank battle 5 miles from Arnhem — Second Army meets stiff opposition — Airborne forces' grim fight — All resistance ended at Boulogne.

'The British Second Army is meeting strong opposition in its battle to reach Arnhem to relieve the British airborne troops, who are facing a critical situation. The nearest point to which the Second Army has penetrated is the village of Elst, five miles from Arnhem

'All organised resistance in Boulogne has ended and the garrison commander and his staff have surrendered.

'The Americans are consolidating their positions in the Siegfried line and Moselle zones, where enemy counter-attacks are increasing in frequency and power...

'The position of the airborne troops at Arnhem, who have been holding out since Sunday against continuous heavy German attacks from all sides, is critical, but with a relief army fighting to reach them it is not hopeless.

'The Germans packed in the territory between Nijmegen and Arnhem to smash allied progress northwards are good-class troops well supplied with anti-tank weapons, and the country over which the British tanks have to travel — flat and with only a few good roads — is well suited to anti-tank gunners.

'Polish airborne reinforcements have joined the Arnhem men and are helping to repel the German attacks. The aircraft in which they travelled were not attacked by the *Luftwaffe*, but another supply air train brought German fighters into the air. In the bad weather the interceptors caused some losses among the supply planes. But these planes were on their way back — they had already dropped their supplies safely.

'Allied fighters and fighter-bombers are giving support to the isolated airborne troops and to the tanks that are fighting hard to break through to them, but bad weather is impeding both the air and ground operations.

'Reinforcements are pouring along the 40-mile-long corridor from the Dutch border to Nijmegen to strengthen General Dempsey's troops and the airborne units with whom they have already linked up and who together are battering slowly northwards...

'The road from Nijmegen northward to Arnhem looks like being a hard one for the British ground troops and American airborne forces who are fighting their way forward against very strong infantry and anti-tank artillery opposition.

'Patrols of our armour have pushed out from the head of our leading column, and their reports indicate that the enemy may break sooner than was expected. The core of the German resistance is at Elst on the road about halfway between Arnhem and Nijmegen...

'Incidentally the Second Army armoured troops south of Arnhem are nearer by many miles to Berlin than any other allied forces, though the destruction of German armies is still the primary aim of the allies rather than the acquisition of enemy territory.' (*The Times*, London, 23.9.1944)

A British pressman's view

A British correspondent with the airborne troops in the Osterbeek perimeter sent home this report at 09.00hrs on the Friday:

'It's a ghastly morning, cold and foggy, and the Germans are shelling us with mortars, heavy artillery and 8.8cm AA guns. The Ack-Ack guns are the most dangerous because you can't hear their shells coming. Some machine-guns have just opened up on our right. In that particular corner of this hell our men are holding houses which are still more or less intact. It is now five days and five sleepness nights since we flew in from Britain. And God knows from what secret source these men draw the strength they need for this interminable battle. One thing is certain: they are going to go on until the Second Army finally gets here. More and more of the Second Army's artillery is supporting us now'.

The previous night the same reporter told his office: 'We've just received copies of today's London papers, dropped to us by parachute.'

The official German summary

On 23 September the German High Command reported:

'Our front north of Arnhem stood firm against heavy enemy pressure north of Arnhem while our own counter-attacks at Vechel drove a wedge between the enemy forces in southern and central Holland. Enemy efforts to extend their bridgehead near Eindhoven have failed and in the fierce fighting which resulted from these efforts the enemy has suffered heavy casualties, In Central Holland 30 enemy tanks have been destroyed.'

Radio Berlin reported the previous evening:

'For the past five days the town of Arnhem has been in flames. One attack follows another. The enemy is fighting desperately while waiting for reinforcements to reach him from the south, where British armoured units are trying to force their way forward across the only bridge which is still standing at Nijmegen. They have made some progress, but a German counter attack from the south-east is imminent.'

A few hours before this announcement the German News Agency had stated that the British 1st Airborne Division, dropped near Arnhem, had been 'completely exterminated'.

The course of the battle

As already described the dropping of the Polish Parachute Brigade had persuaded the Germans to withdraw the powerful Knaust combat group from the Oosterbeek perimeter and thus reduce the pressure on the encircled British. The arrival of the Poles had worried the Germans considerably. They spoke of a 'critical situation' developing because they feared the Poles might move north-east towards the Arnhem bridge and so cut off the Frundsberg Division, which was driving south across the Betuwe plain towards Nijmegen. So Harzer hastily took up a position south of the Rhine on the Betuwe plain between the Arnhem-Nijmegen road and

BRITISH TANKS DRIVING ON TO ARNHEM

◆

ENEMY SHELLED BY SECOND ARMY'S GUNS

RELIEF FOR AIRBORNE FORCE IMMINENT

AACHEN IN RING OF BATTLES

British tanks have crossed the Waal at Nijmegen and are driving northward to link up with the hard-pressed airborne force at Arnhem, on the Lek. Medium artillery of the Second Army was reported early to-day to be shelling targets indicated by the Arnhem force, whose relief is now regarded as imminent.

On both sides of Aachen heavy battles are in progress. In the northern sector American tanks are approaching Geilenkirchen, across the German frontier, and in the south troops are pushing slowly through the Siegfried line east of Stolberg.

The Poles have reached the Scheldt estuary at several points round Terneuzen.

Above left: *Excerpt from* The Times *of 22.9.1944.*
Above right: *Hartenstein Hotel on 24.9.1944: 'The situation is critical but not hopeless.'*
Far left: *Driel: the Poles have landed.*
Left: *Driel: a vehicle of the relieving column arrives at last.*

the Polish landing zone at Driel, determined to keep the Arnhem road open. This redeployment on the Betuwe changed the course of the Arnhem battle. While the Airborne Division struggled for survival north of the river, around the shrinking perimeter a fresh battlefield developed on the Betuwe plain south of the river. Here the Poles and subsequently units of the Second Army trying to get to Oosterbeek had to ward off persistent German assaults.

On Friday morning 22 September a column of British armoured cars, a reconnaissance patrol sent out to find the Poles reached the outposts of the Polish defences at Driel. So Horrocks' ground forces had at last linked up with the 1st Airborne Division. The 48 hours in the schedule of Montgomery's plan had lengthened to four day and 18 hours, and had scarcely achieved the

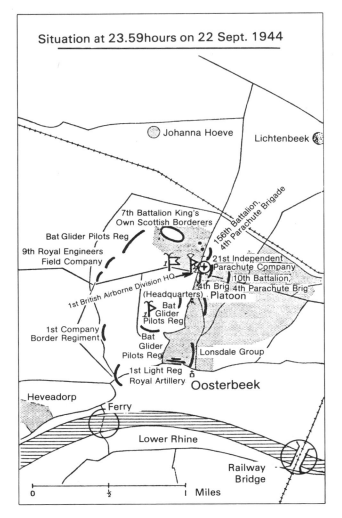

Situation at 23.59 hours on 22 Sept. 1944

Johanna Hoeve   Lichtenbeek

7th Battalion King's
Own Scottish Borderers
Bat Glider Pilots Reg
9th Royal Engineers
Field Company

156th Battalion,
4th Parachute Brigade

21st Independent
Parachute Company
10th Battalion,
4th Parachute Brig
Platoon

1st British Airborne Division HQ
(Headquarters)

Bat
Glider
Pilots Reg

1st Company
Border Regiment

Bat
Glider
Pilots Reg

Lonsdale Group

1st Light Reg
Royal Artillery

Oosterbeek

Heveadorp
Ferry

Lower Rhine

Railway
Bridge

0   ½   1   Miles

promised 'corridor' between the Second Army and the Poles; the passageway was little more than through a sandy path across the flat, low-lying Betuwe.

To reach the Polish enclave the British armoured cars had slipped past the right flank of the Frundsberg Division, which was blocking the main Nijmegen-Arnhem road. Unfortunately, the first armoured car drove over one of the mines which the Poles had laid in front of their positions and a second was soon blown up by another mine. The route across the Betuwe was a tenuous one, but the British managed to hold on to it throughout the battle. It was along this path that the remaining troops in the Oosterbeek perimeter were eventually evacuated safely to Nijmegen.

Inside the perimeter, where the survivors were enduring a round-the-clock bombardment that had steadily increased in weight and fury, the situation was now deteriorating rapidly. The RAF staff turned down an urgent appeal for air support; after serious consideration, they said, they were regretfully unable to comply because of the weather. Worse still, the aircraft due to fly the supplies so urgently required, were unable

to take off. Nevertheless, that day Browning reported to General Eisenhower and General Marshall in Washington that the situation in the Arnhem sector had improved considerably. And when General Smith, commander of the 52nd Infantry Division, offered to put his men into gliders and send them to Uruquhart's aid, Browning signalled back on the Friday morning that though he appreciated the thought it was unnecessary as the situation was better than anticipated.

However, this was the day that the Allied High Command learned the truth about the 1st Airborne Division's plight for the first time. War correspondents at the headquarters of Eisenhower, Brereton and Montgomery were told in confidence that the situation was serious, but that everything was being done to help Uruquhart.

During the evening of 22 September and throughout the night the erosion of the perimeter continued as did the incessant mortaring and shelling. Through a loudspeaker in front of the British positions a voice called on the beleaguered troops to surrender; it quoted British casualty figures and claimed that British officers

Above centre: *Major-General St. Sosabowski* (right).
Above right: *'Red Devils' at Oosterbeek: 'One more river to cross . . .'*
Centre: *'Hells Highway': a burnt out Sherman.*
Below left: *An Allied fighter-bomber, a dreaded foe.*

who had been captured recommended men still in the perimeter to give up the hopeless struggle. The appeal over the strains of *I'm in the Mood for Love* and *One more river to cross* were wafted from the loudspeaker to the paratroops.

At dusk on Friday evening Poles from Driel made their way down to the northern bank of the river since it was planned to ferry supplies to the Oosterbeek pocket. They found the vicinity of the projected crossing swept by unremitting mortar and machine gun fire. Colonel Taylor had been ordered to get supplies to Driel, whence they were to be carried to the 'Red Devils' in two 2½ton amphibious trucks. At midnight the two amphibious vehicles duly set out for the Rhine, but heavy rain during the day had turned the narrow lanes leading to the river bank into a quagmire. Thick fog made the job no easier. To lighten the vehicles some of their freight was jettisoned, but even so they slithered into a ditch only a

few yards from the river bank. There, despite strenuous efforts to free them, the remained stuck. At 03.00hrs the operation was abandoned.

The Poles did not give up the attempt to reinforce the airborne perimeter, however. Next they tried with rubber dinghies and improvised wooden rafts, but most of the rafts proved too cumbersome and the rubber dinghies generally too flimsy. One after another these motley craft were sunk by enemy fire and by dawn only one company of Poles had managed painfully to reach the far bank, having lost about a third of their strength on the crossing. All in all, only 50 soldiers and a negligible amount of supplies finally arrived in Urquhart's perimeter.

Above: *In the perimeter: the supply planes fail to find the dropping zone.*
Right: *A couple of German footsloggers.*

The Seventh Day

23 September 1944

The official Allied summary

Allied Headquarters summarised the events of the weekend on Monday 25 September:

'First link with troops north of Rhine — Supplies ferried across the river — Second Army over the German Frontier — Canadians' 10-mile advance.

'Contact has been made with the British airborne troops isolated north of the Rhine. This first link was made by forces of the Second Army, who crossed the river under cover of darkness in amphibious lorries with food and ammunition.

'The situation was described last night as much brighter, with the Second Army "attacking everywhere" with vigour. They have penetrated a mile into Germany south-east of Nijmegen and captured a village.

'The Canadians have advanced 10 miles across the Escaut canal east of Antwerp in the Turnhout area . . .

'Ducks (amphibious lorries) from the British Second Army crossed the Rhine to-day, carrying ammunition and supplies to the British airborne forces which landed behind the German lines near Arnhem on Sunday last in an attempt to seize the bridge at that point.

'The relief of the beleaguered airborne forces was effected in the nick of time. Food and ammunition were running very low. In the circumstances it is not surprising that nothing further has been heard from the sub-unit of this force which seized the houses dominating the northern end of the Arnhem bridge.

'In very unfavourable weather the R.A.F. has done its best with the American air force to further the great enterprise — the biggest airborne operation ever attempted — but the full degree of support which the operation required has not been possible. Nevertheless great numbers of transport aircraft — tugs, gliders, and troop-carriers — have been making their way over the German lines to bring what help they could to the airborne forces . . .

'There is as yet no news of the Arnhem bridge having been blown, but there is little doubt that the Germans are once more in a position to blow it if they want to. For the time being, however, it would appear that they are anxious to maintain it intact as long as possible . . .

'A powerful enemy counter-attack launched with many tanks yesterday on the west flank of the long snake tongue of our armoured column from the Belgian frontier into Holland cut the road between Eindhoven and Nijmegen. Thus materialised one of the risks deliberately accepted when the British drive began, and the situation created was not a complete surprise.' (*The Times*, London, 25.9.1944)

The official German summary

On Sunday 24 September the German High Command announced: 'The enemy has landed more airborne troops in central Holland, mostly in the south and south-east of the Nijmegen region. Our own forces immediately attacked and heavy fighting is still going on. Our withdrawal from the west of Holland is going according to plan, and southeast of Aachen and on the Eifel front* attacks by the enemy yesterday have all been repulsed . . .'

* *Translator's Note:* This reference is to the Eifel mountains in the Rhineland south of Aachen.

attacks by the enemy yesterday have all been repulsed . . .'

The course of the battle

The weather over England improved on the Saturday and Allied aircraft were at least able to resume operations. But the pilots of the supply-dropping planes could not locate the dropping zone near the Hartenstein Hotel. Heavy anti-aircraft fire brought down six and damaged 63 more of the 123 planes sent on this mission. Once more the 'Red Devils' in the Oosterbeek perimeter had to watch their food and ammunition fall into enemy hands.

In the evening Urquhart radioed to Browning: 'Numerous attacks by infantry, supported by self-propelled guns, tanks and even flamethrowers. All attacks accompanied by heavy shelling and mortaring. Headquarters are also battered. Situation inside the perimeter largely unchanged but positions now more thinly manned. Still no contact with our forces on the south bank. Air supply a failure. Have recovered only a small amount of ammunition. No rations so far. Because of scarcity of water all ranks rather filthy. Morale still high but heavy bombardment is showing signs of effect. Will hold out but looking forward to better days.'

The road to Arnhem and the Zuider Zee through Eindhoven and Nijmegen, by way of which the Second Army was supposed to break through to the Airborne Division, had become known as 'Hell's Highway'. This road was the central axis of the so-called corridor barely a few hundred metres wide in places, which stretched far into enemy territory, and through which the whole of XXX Corps was expected to squeeze. On 23 September 'Hell's Highway' was attacked on both flanks by German forces and only after bitter fighting did the Allies hold open this artery to Nijmegen and the Betuwe.

On Saturday the Germans altered the scheme of their offensive, concentrating their attacks on the north side of the Rhine and directing their thrusts towards the junction of perimeter and river. Harzer knew that the Poles had reached the southern bank and that a division of XXX Corps was trying to break through to the Polish defensive area at Driel. Throughout Saturday, therefore, the stretch of northern river bank which formed part of the Airborne Division's perimeter was subjected to heavy fire from German positions on the east and west flanks.

Another attempt to cross the river had been planned for the Saturday night, when the British 43rd Division was to bring up assault boats for use by the Polish paratroops, while the Divisional artillery provided support and covered the crossing. This time the whole of the Polish Brigade in Driel was to be committed to a desperate effort to reinforce Urquhart's enclave. But just as on the previous night, at about 2200hrs the Poles

Above right: *Excerpt from The Times of 23.9.1944.*
Far right: *Oosterbeek: the Germans try to get around the perimeter and cut it off from the river.*
Right: *Captured 'Red Devil' and SS men.*

TANK BATTLE 5 MILES FROM ARNHEM

——◆——

SECOND ARMY MEETS STIFF OPPOSITION

———

AIRBORNE FORCES' GRIM FIGHT

———

ALL RESISTANCE ENDED AT BOULOGNE

The British Second Army is meeting strong opposition in its battle to reach Arnhem to relieve the British airborne troops, who are facing a critical situation. The nearest point to which the Second Army has penetrated is the village of Elst, five miles from Arnhem.

All organized resistance in Boulogne has ended and the garrison commander and his staff have surrendered.

The Americans are consolidating their positions in the Siegfried line and Moselle zones, where enemy counter-attacks are increasing in frequency and power.

found themselves crouching on the river bank under German shelling waiting for non-existent boats. Their own artillery support was largely ineffective, since the British guns were shooting at maximum range with dubious accuracy. Horrocks had been hoping to ferry British infantrymen over the Rhine as well as Sosabowski's men, but the German artillery thwarted his plans. The first weary men of his 130th Brigade did not arrive at Driel until after nightfall, too late to co-ordinate a crossing with the Poles. In the event, at about 01.00 Sosabowski's paratroops paddled alone across the river in rubber dinghies which the 82nd US Division had brought with them for their operation to capture the bridge at Nijmegen.

Throughout the night the German heavy artillery shelled the river line and the Poles suffered heavy casualties. Of the 250 who eventually got across to the north bank only 200 made it to the perimeter. At sunrise the remainder of the Polish Brigade on the south bank who had been unable to cross the river returned to their positions at Driel. But even now hopes of sending help to the men trapped in the perimeter had not been abandoned.

Above: *Oosterbeek, Weverstraat.*
Centre: *Germans examining a 6-pr anti-tank gun.*
Right: *A British fighter-bomber has been shot down.*

The Eighth Day

24 September 1944

The official German summary

A statement from the German High Command on 25 September reported that:

'In the west of Holland our troops have taken up new positions and driven off several attacks by the enemy. In the Arnhem-Nijmegen area the enemy airborne troops have not had an opportunity to concentrate for a major assault and they have suffered further heavy losses from our counter-attack. Bitter hand-to-hand fighting developed when the enemy attempted to consolidate his positions. Another 800 wounded hemmed into a tiny area west of Arnhem have been captured; these men were part of what remains of the British 1st Airborne Division. East of Eindhoven the enemy has gained some ground. Despite bad weather our fighter-bombers have successfully supported our ground troops. North and south-east of Aachen enemy attacks have been repulsed and several enemy tanks have been destroyed. On the Eifel front the enemy has lost sixteen tanks in fruitless assaults.

The course of the battle

Throughout Sunday German artillery hammered the perimeter. 'The smaller the perimeter gets', remarked Harzer, the more obstinately the British troops fight for every inch and inch of ground.' In spite of heavy losses, the RAF tried yet again to drop supplies into the perimeter, but once more almost all the containers landed behind the German lines.

In Driel, too, the mortaring and shelling intensified during the day and the buildings housing the Polish (Parachute) Field Ambulance were frequently hit. A third attempt to ferry troops across the river was laid on that night. The 5th Bn The Dorset Regiment of the 43rd Division were to cross first, then the Polish Brigade. At 2200hrs the Corps artillery launched a massive bombardment of the German positions along the Rhine. The assault troops had to huddle in rain and cold for three hours until the vehicles carrying assault boats eventually pulled into Driel at midnight. Only nine trucks turned up; the others had wound up in enemy territory near Elst. On the road down to the river two of the nine slid off the road into a dike and stuck in the mud. Then is was discovered that no oars had been sent up with the boats. The British finished up carrying the boats across the last half a kilometre of swampy ground to the river, and losing a precious hour in the process. Just as they were about to launch the boats, one was set on fire by a shell and a second was riddled by fragments from another shell. Murderous machine-gun fire from the far bank raked the river and burning buildings threw the wooded slope of the Westerbowing hill into clear y-lit relief. Nevertheless the boats were launched; but some were promptly swept away by the swiftly flowing river, so the Poles handed over their boats to the British as replacements.

At 03.30hrs on the Monday morning another attempt to get supplies across the river was mounted. Six amphibious trucks were brought up, but only three made it to the water; the drivers of the other three found the bank too steep to manoeuvre their wide, cumbersome vehicles. The three which did get into the water crossed

FIRST LINK WITH TROOPS NORTH OF RHINE

---◆---

SUPPLIES FERRIED ACROSS THE RIVER

SECOND ARMY OVER THE GERMAN FRONTIER

CANADIANS' 10-MILE ADVANCE

Contact has been made with the British airborne troops isolated north of the Rhine. This first link was made by forces of the Second Army, who crossed the river under cover of darkness in amphibious lorries with food and ammunition.

The situation was described last night as much brighter, with the Second Army "attacking everywhere" with vigour. They have penetrated a mile into Germany south-east of Nijmegen and captured a village.

The Canadians have advanced 10 miles across the Escaut canal east of Antwerp in the Turnhout area.

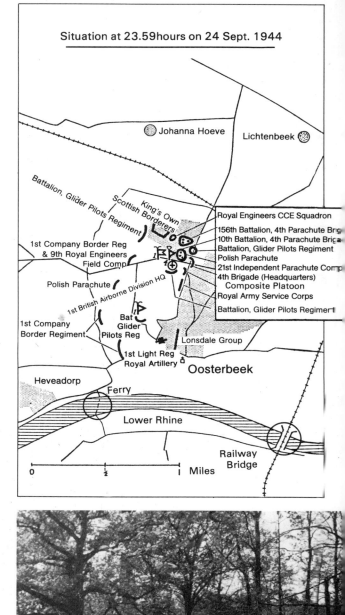

Situation at 23.59hours on 24 Sept. 1944

Johanna Hoeve
Lichtenbeek

Battalion, Glider Pilots Regiment
King's Own Scottish Borderers
1st Company Border Reg & 9th Royal Engineers Field Comp.
Polish Parachute
1st British Airborne Division HQ
1st Company Border Regiment
Bat Glider Pilots Reg
1st Light Reg Royal Artillery
Lonsdale Group
Oosterbeek
Heveadorp
Ferry
Lower Rhine
Railway Bridge
0   ½   1   Miles

Royal Engineers CCE Squadron
156th Battalion, 4th Parachute Brig
10th Battalion, 4th Parachute Briga
Battalion, Glider Pilots Regiment
Polish Parachute
21st Independent Parachute Comp
4th Brigade (Headquarters)
Composite Platoon
Royal Army Service Corps
Battalion, Glider Pilots Regiment

to the far side without much difficulty, but then they all bogged down helplessly in the mud on the opposite bank. At dawn, enemy fire quickly brought down the curtain on this final, desperate attempt to supply the airborne troops in the perimeter.

All this time efforts to get men across the river were continuing. But at first light around 04.00hrs, no more than a hundred or so British soldiers had succeeded in getting across and at sunrise the remainder, carrying three wounded men with them, retired to Driel to rejoin the Poles.

Above left: *Excerpt from* The Times *of 25.9.1944.*
Above right: *Captured Polish paratroop officers: only 200 men got to the perimeter.*
Right: *Inside the Oosterbeek perimeter.*
Far right: *Oosterbeek, British prisoners: the battle is nearing its end.*

Above and right: Allied Bren carriers in the Arnhem region: the relieving force is halted by a counter-attack.

100

The Ninth Day

25 September 1944

The official Allied summary

On Tuesday 26 September Allied Headquarters reported the previous day's fighting thus:

'Second Army's battle of the corridor — Germans driven off road — More air support for troops near Arnhem — Canadian gains at Calais.

'It was stated at midnight that the British corridor through Holland to the Lower Rhine was open again after it had been cut for several hours in a night attack by SS troops.

'Supplies are again flowing north in the direction of Arnhem and the airborne troops north of the Rhine yesterday received stronger support from the air.

'Smalls number of British infantry crossed the lower Rhine yesterday, but no further link up with the airborne troops west of Arnhem was reported...

'The grim fight of the British and Polish airborne troops in and around Arnhem goes on, but, though their situation now is admittedly critical, it is not yet hopeless.

'More reinforcements reached them across the river south of the town during the night, with a certain amount of supplies. On the road up from the south the town of E st, where German opposition to our advance has been fiercest, there were few signs of the enemy last night, but it is possible that the place is clear by now.

'The scanty reports so far received from our airborne men indicate that they are getting very tired and enduring punishing mortar and shell fire, but some of them have added the comment that this is the Germans' last defensive position in this region.' (*The Times* London, 26.9.1944)

The official German summary

The German High Command statement of Tuesday 26 September ran:

'In central Holland, particularly around Eindhoven, the bitter fighting is continuing. Attacks south-west of Vechel have been repulsed, but south and south-east of Helmond the enemy has been able to advance eastwards some kilometres. An attempt to relieve the encircled remnants of the 1st Airborne Division has been smashed and the enemy has suffered heavy casualties. North of Arnhem British armoured columns attempted to push forward, but they have gained little ground. Despite adverse weather conditions our fighter-bombers have successfully attacked enemy troop concentrations, infantry positions and river-crossing activities south-east of Arnhem. In these operations the enemy has again suffered heavy casualties and lost 23 planes in air battles.... In minor actions south-east of Aachen several enemy assaults have been driven back and one American combat group has been encircled.'

The course of the battle

At 06.05hrs on 25 September Urquhart, having heard from Major-General Thomas, commander of the 43rd Division, that it had been decided the Second Army should remain on the south bank of the river and not attempt any more crossings, prepared to withdraw and about three hours later, at 09.30hrs, Montgomery confirmed the order to pull out. Some humorist code-named the withdrawal 'Operation Berlin'.

At 21.00hrs the artillery of the 43rd Division opened

SECOND ARMY'S BATTLE OF THE CORRIDOR

◆

GERMANS DRIVEN OFF ROAD

MORE AIR SUPPORT FOR TROOPS NEAR ARNHEM

CANADIAN GAINS AT CALAIS

It was stated at midnight that the British corridor through Holland to the Lower Rhine was open again after it had been cut for several hours in a night attack by S.S. troops.

Supplies are again flowing north in the direction of Arnhem, and the airborne troops north of the Rhine yesterday received stronger support from the air.

Small numbers of British infantry crossed the lower Rhine yesterday, but no further link up with the airborne troops west of Arnhem was reported.

Canadian troops, supported by British artillery, yesterday began an all-out assault on Calais after the port had been heavily bombed by the R.A.F. In some places the outer defences have been overrun.

up from the Betuwe plain on the German positions flanking the perimeter and under cover of the barrage boats were carried down to the river. The first of them was launched at 21.40hrs and the evacuation began soon after. Operation Market Garden had ended; Operation Berlin had begun.

Above left: *Excerpt from* The Times *of 26.9.1944.*
Above right, right and far right: *a German ambulance convoy has been shot to pieces.*

Above: *German paratroops on the fringe of the British perimeter: 'the situation in Arnhem is grave'.*
Right: *The British war correspondent Alan Wood inside the perimeter.*

The Tenth Day

26 September 1944

The Official Allied summary

On Wednesday, 27 September Allied Headquarters reported the previous day's fighting as follows:

'Second Army's corridor widened — Advances on both flanks — Fleet of air transports lands men and supplies — Enemy forces hemmed in at Calais.

'General Dempsey has secured more room to manoeuvre by the widening and strengthening of the Second Army's corridor in Holland. Advances have been made on both flanks.

'Reinforcements and supplies were flown into the corridor yesterday by a fleet of transports.

'There is no news of the airborne forces at and west of Arnhem, and their situation is thought to be very grave...

'Sufficient progress has been made in the thickening of the right flank of our advance towards the lower Rhine to bring a supplementary route into use pending the dislodgement of the Germans sitting on the main road from Eindhoven to Nijmegen. The right flank troops have in fact moved up from Deurne as far as Oplo, against opposition that was strong in parts but not consistently strong... (*The Times*, London, 27.9.1944)

In the issue of 27 September the London *Times* also reported:

The situation at and west of Arnhem is very grave, whether or not there is truth in the German statement that the last survivors of the British 1st Airborne Division have surrendered. The British Second Army has hitherto been unable to secure a firm grip on the south bank of the lower Rhine, so that there never was a firm link with the airborne forces beyond it.

'Between the Waal and the lower Rhine there is nothing so ugly as this to record, but even here affairs cannot be described as wholly propitious. A German counter-thrust has put the enemy in possession of Elst, on the direct road from Nijmegen to Arnhem. Fortunately there are other routes.

'The long corridor must be subject to German incursions, but south of the Waal matters are now better, and it seems that even if the enemy can on occasion break in it may be expected that he will always be forced out again.'

The official German summary

On Wednesday 27 September 1944 the German High Command reported:

'In the Arnhem area all organised resistance by the British 1st Airborne Division was overcome on 26 September. Thus, despite its fierce resistance and the fact that airborne reinforcements were dropped to it, an elite British division had been completely destroyed by an improvised Wehrmacht force, hurriedly concentrated under the command of an SS-Panzer Korps general, SS Obergruppenführer Bittrich. Every attempt to relieve the encircled division was defeated and the enemy suffered heavy losses. A total of 6450 prisoners has been taken, and thousands of dead have been counted; 30 anti-tank guns, numerous other guns and weapons together with 250 vehicles have also been captured. Additionally a thousand gliders have been destroyed or captured and over a hundred planes have been shot down. Bitter

SECOND ARMY'S CORRIDOR WIDENED

ADVANCES ON BOTH FLANKS

FLEET OF AIR TRANSPORTS LANDS MEN AND SUPPLIES

ENEMY FORCES HEMMED IN AT CALAIS

General Dempsey has secured more room to manoeuvre by the widening and strengthening of the Second Army's corridor in Holland. Advances have been made on both flanks.

Reinforcements and supplies were flown into the corridor yesterday by a fleet of transports.

There is no news of the airborne forces at and west of Arnhem, and their situation is thought to be very grave.

At Calais the Canadians are progressing satisfactorily, and the main body of the enemy garrison has been pushed back into the town itself.

fighting has continued in the Eindhoven region, where the British have reinforced and re-supplied by air. North and east of Nijmegen enemy attacks have been repulsed. On the entire Aachen front, as far south as Metz, there has been only minor activity and sporadic artillery fire by both sides.'

Above left: *Excerpt from* The Times *of 27.9.1944.*
Above centre: *Oosterbeek on the morning of 26.9.44. The enemy has gone.*
Above right: *Parabolas of German tracer photographed as the British withdraw.*
Below right: *The evacuation of the perimeter starts at about 22.00hrs: German armoured cars in action.*
Overleaf above: *After the battle: German guns pull out.*
Overleaf below: *Nijmegen: survivors of the 1st Airborne Division.*

Epilogue

On Thursday 28 September Allied Headquarters announced that Operation Market Garden had been concluded. This was how it was reported:

'2,000 men return from Arnhem — Last of Airborne division withdrawn — Troops ferried across Rhine by night — Broadening front on Maas.

'The troops of the British 1st Airborne Division who could be withdrawn were brought back across the lower Rhine on Monday and Tuesday night after making their gallant stand in the Arnhem area since September 17.

'The number of the division dropped for the operation, not counting several hundred glider pilots, was about 6,500, and of these about 2,000 have returned unwounded. Twelve hundred wounded men have had to be left behind, but an officer who has escaped since the evacuation has reported that the Germans were treating them with consideration.

'The corridor of the Second Army's northward advance into Holland is being steadily widened, and on the right flank general progress is being made towards the line of the Maas...

'The troops of the British 1st Airborne Division who could be withdrawn across the lower Rhine have been brought back, and that part of the operation is at an end. The withdrawal was carried out mainly on Monday night, but also on Tuesday night.

'It appears to be considered that the factor which just tipped the balance over to failure in this one section of General Dempsey's great enterprise — otherwise wholly successful up to date — was the peculiarly bad weather which prevented the dropping of adequate supplies and reinforcements and also facilitated the German counterattacks. The margin was certainly a small one.

'This heroic action for the Arnhem bridgehead, one which will rank among the most outstanding of the war, has deservedly caught the attention of the whole country, including those people who do not commonly go deep into the detail of military operations. The sacrifices of our troops and their inability to put the final touch of success to their magnificent achievement have caused regret and disappointment.

'That is natural, but it would be wrong for us to allow the fact to be obscured that the greater part of the bold enterprise succeeded. What has been gained is a considerable asset. Moreover, the fight put up by the 1st Airborne Division made a powerful contribution to the success in other parts of the corridor, notably at the Nijmegen bridge.

'For the time being the enemy has abandoned his attempts to cut the corridor, and there is a prospect that it will soon be greatly thickened by the movements now in progress on its flanks. But the obstacle of the lower Rhine remains to be overcome, and it must be accepted that the enemy will have by now done much to consolidate its defence.' (*The Times*, London, 28.9.1944)

The following message was dispatched on Tuesday from a correspondent of the combined British Press with the Arnhem airborne force:-

'This is the end. The most tragic and glorious battle of the war is over, and the survivors of this British airborne force can sleep soundly for the first time in eight days and nights.' (*The Times*, London, 28.9.1944)

'The German news agency yesterday issued these figures of losses said to have been inflicted on the allied airborne division in the Arnhem area:- Prisoners, 6,450, including 1,700 wounded; killed, over 1,500. It also claimed that 250 lorries, 30 anti-tank guns, and 250 transport gliders were captured, and 719 transport gliders destroyed.—*Reuter*.' (*The Times*, London, 28.9.1944)

The course of the battle

The plan drawn up by Urquhart's staff envisaged a phased withdrawal from the perimeter. The positions in the northernmost corner of the pocket would be evacuated first; then the withdrawal would gradually progress southwards, so that the men nearest the river bank would be the last to leave. As the rearguard thinned out, the men who remained were to continue firing to persuade the Germans that there had been no change within the perimeter. Two routes to the Rhine, at the eastern and western extremities of the escape corridor, had been reconnoitred on Monday evening; the paths were unobtrusively marked and glider pilots were posted as guides.

Responsibility for organisation of the river crossing was handed to the Sappers, using assault boats that could take 14 soldiers apiece. Sentries were detailed to remain with the German prisoners held in the perimeter until a few minutes before the evacuation was complete, so as to ensure that the enemy did not get wind of the withdrawal until it was too late for them to react. Urquhart decided that his ADMS (Assistant Director of Medical Services, i.e. the Division's chief doctor) and the medical personnel should stay behind with the wounded and go into captivity with them*.

The withdrawal got under way about 22.00hrs, in a pitch darkness and pelting rain; the only light came from burning houses and exploding artillery shells. Sergeant O. B. Rees, one of the last to leave the perimeter, recalls: 'that afternoon, the signal officer had managed to pick up bits of the BBC news which said that the Second Army was getting near Arnhem. Everybody knew they couldn't possibly leave us to our fate. Our perimeter had shrunk to about 1500 by 900yds and it was under incessant fire. There wasn't a safe corner anywhere. The cellars of the nearby houses were full of wounded and the dead were laid out in rows on the lawns. We couldn't bury any more of them. We'd been nearly eight nights now without sleep and we didn't have a thing — no ammunition, no dressings and no food. At least we had something to drink, because we collected rainwater in our ground sheets. About 1800hrs the lieutenant told us we were going to evacuate the perimeter that night, because strong German resistance had prevented the Second Army to come to our help. All our equipment, apart from what we could stuff in our haversacks, was to

---

* *Translator's note:* To a man the doctors volunteered to stay.

110

2,000 MEN RETURN FROM ARNHEM

◆

LAST OF AIRBORNE DIVISION WITHDRAWN

TROOPS FERRIED ACROSS RHINE BY NIGHT

BROADENING FRONT ON MAAS

The troops of the British 1st Airborne Division who could be withdrawn were brought back across the lower Rhine on Monday and Tuesday night after making their gallant stand in the Arnhem area since September 17.

The number of the division dropped for the operation, not counting several hundred glider pilots, was about 6,500, and of these about 2,000 have returned unwounded. Twelve hundred wounded men have had to be left behind, but an officer who has escaped since the evacuation has reported that the Germans were treating them with consideration.

The corridor of the Second Army's northward advance into Holland is being steadily widened, and on the right flank general progress is being made towards the line of the Maas.

---

be destroyed. We tied strips of blanket round our boots so as to be able to sneak past the German positions without making too much noise.

'We climbed out of our slit-trenches soon after 22.00hrs. An ear-splitting barrage was going on at the time and our lads shot off what was left of their own ammunition so that it wouldn't fall into enemy hands. With each of us holding on to the jacket of the man in front, our ghostly column sneaked down the path between the trees, full of leaves and branches. After we'd gone about 200yds we were in the middle of the enemy positions, and it didn't feel too good to know we could be shot up from any direction. But we had orders to continue walking even if we were fired on: if anybody was hit, the man behind was supposed to carry him along.

'I could just make out the outline of the man in front of me. All I knew about him was that I was holding the back of his smock. For the first time in my life I was grateful that the rain was coming down in buckets, because it drowned any noise we were making. At each bend of the path there was a glider pilot standing like a shadow. We halted several times, and each time I landed up with my nose on the back of the man in front. When

the lads at the head of the column had made sure the path was free we carried on. Once we had to stop because one of the lads got a bullet in his leg. We wanted to carry him piggyback, but he whispered 'Shut up — just give me a field dressing and it'll be OK. I can walk.'

'Eventually we got through the trees. Until then we'd followed carefully chosen tracks, but now we had to cross flat meadowland at the end of which, somewhere in the dark, was the river. We could hear the water churning up front, while we watched the tracer behind us arcing in a whole range of parabolas depending on the calibre of the gun it came from.

'For a good two hours, we lay in a ditch full of rainwater at the edge of the field, until sometime after midnight a runner arrived with a message to say it was our turn. We only had to get to the far side of the field and then crawl over the dike. But suddenly mortar fire rained down along the river line. I was worried about those who had already got to the river's edge. Anyway, we took a chance and crawled across the muddy ground towards the Rhine. Then we spotted the silhouette of an assault craft in the darkness. To get to it we had to wade into the river up to our waists, urged on by a Canadian sapper in the back of the boat who was shouting "Get a move on, boys, it's not very healthy here!". We helped to push the boat out into the fast-flowing stream, then

Above left: *Excerpt from* The Times *of 28.9.1944.*
111
Top: *Nijmegen: the men who made it.*
Above: *Survivors: Major R. T. H. Lonsdale from Ireland* (left)*, Lt D. A. Dolley of London* (right) *in Nijmegen.*

Oosterbeek perimeter: '. . . . the battle was a decided victory . . .'

crouched down in it, head between knees and squeezed together like sardines in a tin. I was waiting for us to stop a shell or something similar from the opposite side, but nothing happened, though plenty of shells whistled over our heads. A sharp jolt and the trip was over. We climbed out and followed a white tape up the dike bank on all fours, then just slid down the far side, on our bottoms. Now we had to trot through about 4½ miles of ankle-deep mud, all the time in earshot of the racket still going on around the river. I kept thinking: "You're still alive, boy — how in hell did you manage it?"

'Somewhere we came to a barn, with a Red Cross flag where we got a cup of tea with some rum in it and a warm blanket to wrap round our shoulders. But then we had to go on walking all through the night until, absolutely dead tired, we reached a field hospital just outside Nijmegen.'

Others who escaped to the south of the river did not fare so well. There were not enough vehicles to carry everyone on to Nijmegen, so some of the men, including a few wounded, still had a long muddy walk to Nijmegen ahead of them.

After the last boat had gone, hundreds of helpless soldiers were still crouching in the pouring rain and under fire on the northern bank. Two or three boats tried to get back across the Rhine under cover of a smoke screen, but the evacuation had to be stopped at dawn and the wounded dragged themselves back to the field hospitals which had by this time been taken over by the Germans. By 09.00hrs on Tuesday morning the shooting had stopped and the battlefield at Oosterbeek was silent.

Operation Market Garden was over. The weather, which has been consistently bad since 18 September, the second day of the operation, took much of the blame because it prevented the anticipated air support. Unexpected and determined German resistance was advanced as another reason for failure, and some made Sosabowski a scapegoat for the course the operations had taken in the Arnhem area. Gen Browning complained to his superiors that, while every unit in the British Second Army had had to contend with great difficulties in trying to relieve the 1st Airborne Division near Arnhem, Sosabowski had shown absolutely no understanding of the urgency the operation dictated. As a result, Sosabowski was relieved of command of the 1st Polish Independent Parachute Brigade; the Court of Inquiry which he demanded to clear his name was never convened.

Wrote Churchill:

'It was not till I returned from Canada, where the glorious reports had flowed in, that I was able to understand all that had happened. General Smuts was grieved at what seemed to be a failure, and I telegraphed: ". . . As regards Arnhem, I think you have got the position a little out of focus. The battle was a decided victory, but the leading division, asking, quite rightly, for more, was given a chop. I have not been afflicted by any feeling of disappointment over this and am glad our commanders are capable of running this kind of risk.'

Winston Churchill, 9 October 1944